Entrepreneurship That Makes Cents

Empowering entrepreneurs to live life on purpose!

Mike Raber

Quantity order requests can be emailed to:
publishing@rejilaberje.com
Or mailed to:
Reji Laberje Author Programs
Publishing Orders
234 W. Broadway Street
Waukesha, WI 53186

Raber, Mike
Entrepreneurship That Makes Cents
Contributing Editor: RaeAnne Scargall
Cover Design & Interior Layout: Michael Nicloy

ISBN: 069267165X
ISBN-13: 978-0692671658
BISAC Codes:
BUSINESS & ECONOMICS / Personal Finance / Money Management-BUS050030
BUSINESS & ECONOMICS / Industries / Financial Services-BUS070140
BUSINESS & ECONOMICS / Mentoring & Coaching-BUS106000

Writing and Publishing
www.rejilaberje.com

I dedicate this book to all of the many mentors I have been blessed to work with over the years and to Jennifer for being a loving, supportive mother and wife. I hope that this book will serve as a powerful tool to help you take your business to the next level and beyond.

Table of Contents

Foreword

Entrepreneurship That Makes Cents is a Reji Laberje Author Programs interactive text. The QR code below will provide a little more insight about Mike Raber and what he has to share, including resources and the tables and charts found within this book, on the Electronic Resource Hub (ERH).

Find a free QR scanner for your smart device via a search through your device's app store. Then, you can scan the QR code with your smart device to discover the ERH online.
Find more information at:
www.entrepreneurshipthatmakescents.com

Try it out now by scanning the QR code:

Acknowledgements

The creation of this book has been a culmination of a lifelong dream to empower people to live their lives on purpose. Over the years, as I continued to develop and bring my dream into realty, it took the help of many great mentors. They helped keep me on track when I would lose faith or focus, and they helped to shape the man and father I have become. This book is the first of many great resources geared to help entrepreneurs build a successful business with a solid foundation. There are many people I want to thank, starting with my own family for teaching me the value and belief that I can do anything I put my mind to. That belief gave me the strength to continue on when many of the people around me told me I was crazy for having such a dream.

I would also like to give a special thanks to Brian Buffini and everyone at Buffini and Company. Without their help over the years, we probably would have lost our business, and perhaps worse. Due to all of your help over the years, my daughter Sabrina and I have been able to teach hundreds of children how to save, share, and spend their money wisely. It is from all your teachings that I was able to write this book. I will be forever grateful.

I would highly recommend that you also go to www.buffiniandcompany.com and check out their training and coaching systems. They have truly allowed us to build great businesses that have impacted and improved the lives of our family and those of hundreds of our clients.

By ourselves we can do great things, yet together we can climb the highest mountains.

Entrepreneurship That Makes Cents

SECTION ONE

THE BEGINNING

TURNING A DREAM INTO A PROFITABLE BUSINESS

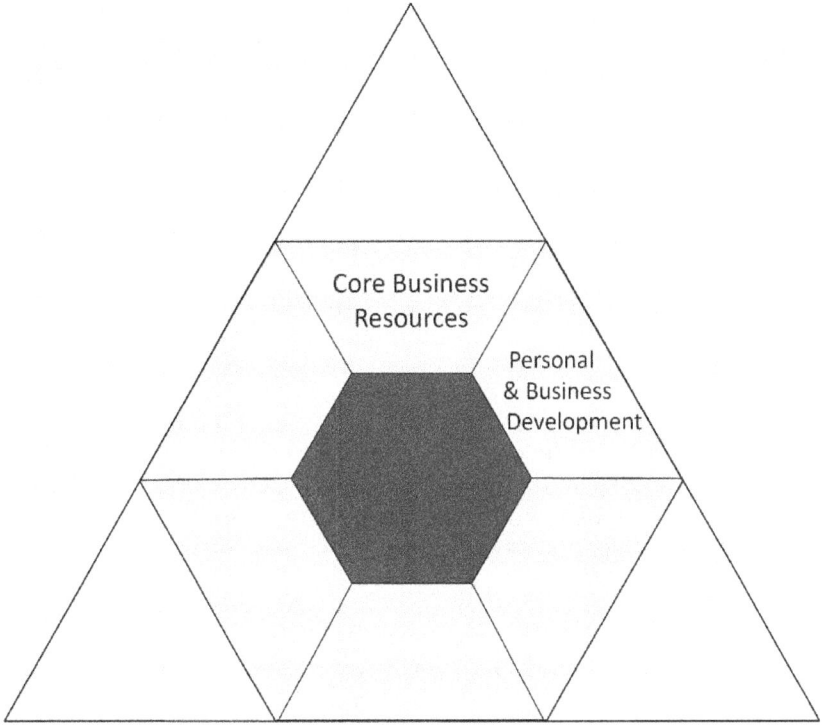

Core Business
Resources

Personal
& Business
Development

CHAPTER 1:
INTRODUCTION

Welcome to Centsible Solutions. Why is "Sensible" spelled "Centsible"? It's a play on words: Centsible or Cent-sible, as in dollars and cents. Centsible Solutions is the branding for a series of books and training programs that we are writing and creating. Later in this book, there is a chapter on creating a brand or brand name for your business that will explain more. But for now, think of Centsible Solutions as your financial and business concierge.

The mission of Centsible Solutions is to empower entrepreneurs to reach their full potentials while bringing their dreams to life. Whether you want to start a new business or build an existing business, we will help you take your business to the next level!

We believe people are created to reach great heights, yet oftentimes they need to be encouraged and guided through the process. So, we designed a community named Centsible Connections that comprises likeminded professionals and entrepreneurs who work together to help each other succeed. We hope to serve as the cornerstone between our members and their clients and customers.

We provide efficient and friendly solutions to entrepreneurs that empower them to build great businesses through leveraging their time, lead generation activities, and skill sets. We continually provide a combination of continued support, marketing, business and personal training, and the core business resources needed to grow a vibrant business.

I have found that many small-business owners try to become sufficient in many different areas, yet they end up not doing very well in any of them. True champions focus on what they do best and surround themselves with others whose strengths are their weaknesses, through delegating activities to other professionals (instead of, for example, prematurely hiring employees or spending time doing less efficient activities).

I believe that as a business grows, it's important to develop a team of outside advisors or mentors to network with and have as a resource to assist with more complex projects. True, you may be in business for yourself, but you should never be entirely by yourself. In today's high-tech world, a business is only as strong as the foundational systems and employees that are in place to run it.

Over years of working with many different types of clients, I have found that successful businesspeople have developed a consistent combination of a

- Healthy mindset
- Healthy physical habits
- Healthy financial fundamentals

It's very important for entrepreneurs to continually evolve in these three areas. In order to reach their true potential, they must continue to grow and develop healthy mindsets. If they are not physically healthy, they will not have the energy needed to grow their businesses. If their financial foundations are weak, they will be under a great deal of stress—and run the risk of ultimately stunting growth or collapsing a business.

I have found that successful businesspeople have learned how to continually grow and refine these three areas. When building a business, the effectiveness, efficiency, and level of refinement will determine the degree of growth the business will experience. When the three areas are not working in harmony, the business will not run efficiently, like a table missing a leg. On the next page is a list of other core areas entrepreneurs should continue to grow in.

Personal/Spiritual Development - Creating an Abundance Mindset
- ✓ Personal and spiritual growth
- ✓ Goal-setting/dream-building: finding your passion
- ✓ Learning to let go: creating contentment, peace, and joy
- ✓ Social events/fellowship and fun actives

Physical/Health and Wellness - Creating a Healthy Lifestyle
- ✓ Proper nutrition: developing healthy eating habits
- ✓ Effective exercise: recharging your energy level

Wealth Management Solutions - Creating a Proactive Financial Life Plan
- ✓ Cash flow and net worth analysis
- ✓ Creating a solid financial foundation
- ✓ Proper protection: life, health, business, long-term care, disability
- ✓ Debt-management: creating healthy spending habits
- ✓ Asset accumulation/wealth preservation and estate planning

Business Development, Mentoring, & Coaching - Creating Accountability in Your Business
- ✓ Business development, systems, and support
- ✓ Becoming part of a mastermind alliance

Personal & Business Development Resources
- ✓ A leadership team: a team of industry experts that can act as a temporary board of directors

Financial Planning Resources
- ✓ Cash flow management
- ✓ Net worth tracking
- ✓ Investment solutions

Business Administration - The Day-to-Day Running of Your Business

- ✓ Client-coordination services
- ✓ Computer and I.T. services: computer implementation and repair
- ✓ Human resources: hiring, payroll, employee procedures manuals
- ✓ Employee Benefits: 401K, HSA, HRA-105 Plan, etc.
- ✓ Insurance: property, key person, life, health, errors and omission, labor and industry, umbrella polices, the list goes on...
- ✓ Legal team: a general business or contract attorney that can help with business setup, creating trademarks, patents, or copyrights

Lead Generation
- ✓ Marketing/graphic arts: creating logos, personal brand marketing material, and maintaining a web presence
- ✓ Marketing (personal/non-personal promotion)
- ✓ Database management

A strong systematized database is a key asset needed for the growth of a business, yet it is often the most neglected. I have found that entrepreneurs will often spend a large amount of money and time trying to acquire leads to fill their pipeline, but once they get busy, they will neglect the very things that brought business in the door, creating peaks and valleys in the day-to-day operations of the business. As you begin to develop your database and implement the systems that I will cover throughout this book, you will begin to experience the following benefits:

1. As you prioritize and grow your database, it will turn into a walking, talking billboard—in essence, it will create ambassadors that will become your greatest advocates for your business.
2. A reduction in your risks will develop when you create a community within your database, and your business will take on a life of its own.
3. You will minimize your marketing expense. Through the power of the referral system, as your clients become true ambassadors for your business, they will refer people to you on a regular basis. This will allow you to focus on the needs of your clients, rather than spending a lot of time, money, and effort on advertising. Two of the biggest potential pitfalls that a new business will face are either blowing its marketing budget or failing to market at all. At the end of the day, the true value of a business is in the quality of relationships within its database.

"There is one quality which one must possess to win, and that is the definiteness of purpose, the knowledge of what one wants, and a burning desire to possess it."
— Napoleon Hill

CHAPTER 2:
DEFINING YOUR "WHY"

All great things must start with a first step.

My "why" began at age twelve:

I saw a need and set out to meet it!
I saw a solution and set out to find it!
I had a vision and set out to create it!

All great businesses start as an idea or a dream. Over time, that dream can grow into a business. The goal of this book is to help you lay the foundation for your dream or idea and transform it into a fully living, self-sustaining business that will be around for many years to come. The strength of a solid business foundation depends on many variables, such as the skill sets or expertise of the owners, the people they are around, the marketability of their idea, and the cash reserves available to them.

Let's begin with a few questions:

What is it that you are truly passionate about?

_____

_____

When you envision your dream business, what does it really look like?

_____

_____

If success were absolutely guaranteed, what would your business look like?

_____

_____

After years of working with business owners from all walks of life, I have found that most of them didn't just wake up one day with a dream or vision to go out and start a business. Some had an idea or vision of something that could be "done better." Others had a dream to build something great, and over time, that dream became clearer. Others experienced a lifestyle change, or lost a job and found themselves back on the market. Often, these individuals have a large amount of experience and not many (if any) opportunities to do what they did before. People are often unable to find a job that will pay them what they deserve or made before they got laid off. And, many times, these people find that they are forced to recreate themselves.

Then there are those who get sick of working for someone else and decide to take their skills to the open market, like a plumber who decides to buy a van, a bunch of tools, and goes into business for him- or herself. In Michael Gerber's book *The E-Myth,* he refers to this type of person as a "technician suffering from an entrepreneur's seizure."

The challenge most people face is that they think they are going into business for themselves; however, they are really just buying a job. Yes, they may work for themselves, but if they don't go out and do whatever it is that they do—the plumber doesn't fix someone's pipes—they won't have any income coming in. Dean Fliss, one of my mentors, often says, "The value of a business is what it will produce without you in it."

Let's go back to talking about your dream, or why you want to open a business or become an entrepreneur. Building a business can be very rewarding, yet it can be one of the more difficult things you will do in your life. So, the stronger your "Why," the easier it will be to overcome challenges as they arise.

In his book *Start with Why*, Simon Sinek talks about how people get so focused on the how or what they do that they forget why they decided to go into business in the first place. Again, what is the purpose or mission behind your business? The answer to this question will give you the strength to persevere when faced with adversity.

People may need what you do or sell, but it's the passion behind why you do it that usually closes the sale. In the end, people are attracted to why you do it. How strong is your "Why"? Do other people get excited when you tell them what it is you do and why you do it? Do you get excited when you talk about it? What is it about your business that you're passionate about? Why did you start your business in the first place? Why did you pick the product you sell or the service you provide? It's the answers to these questions that will engage your passion and purpose for being in business.

There will be times when you'll want to quit and run for the hills. It's your passion or "Why" that will get you through the hard times. Brian Buffini, a mentor of mine, would often say, "If your *why* is strong enough, you can endure any *how*."

So, I ask you: are you a true entrepreneur, or a technician with an entrepreneur's seizure? The answer to this question will determine the types of systems you will need to run your business. Are you more of a thinker or creator? Or are you more of a worker bee? If you had a bakery, would you rather spend your day baking cakes or coming up with new recipes and places you can market them? Do you see yourself making a predetermined amount of cakes to sell each day? Or do you want to sell as many cakes as you possibly can and open multiple bakeries across town or around the country? A business needs both types of people; however, both will require different skill sets. A strong business will have both types of people in it. In other words, do your goals for the business reach beyond the service or products that the business sells?

When I was running a business called Newcastle Limousine, my goal wasn't to have the newest and coolest fleet—although I had one of the newest fleets in the city. My goal wasn't to offer the most services at the lowest prices, although my prices were very competitive. My goal was to impact and improve the lives of my clients. I wanted every person who got into one of our cars to be in a better place when he or she got out.

I would often get referrals and testimonies from clients for helping them in ways that had nothing to do with transportation or even the limousine industry. My goal was to make my clients feel like they were my *only* client.

Back when Krispy Kreme first opened in Seattle, it was common for customers to have to wait in line for two to three hours to buy donuts. There were times when I would be finishing a job and passing Krispy Kreme around three o'clock in the morning. At that time of the day there wouldn't be any line, so I would pop in and buy a few dozen donuts. I would then deliver them to my clients who weren't able to get out until much later in the morning.

One such morning, I stopped by a client's house. She was not at home, so I left the donuts and a quick note with her daughter. The note read, "Hi, Ginene. I know that you've probably heard about this new donut place and how long their lines are. They have great donuts, and I wanted you to be able to try them. I value you as a friend and client and hope that you have a great day."

Later that day, I received a phone call from her. Her voice was cracking as she said, "Thank you so much for the donuts. Today was my birthday, and the only two people who validated it were my daughter and you. Thank you so much!" That day I made a difference in her life, not because I picked her up in a shiny new car, but because I showed her that I valued her as a person and met a need far deeper than a ride to the airport.

I will share many stories throughout this book about the benefits that can come from starting and growing a business, even if it's just a small business or something you do on the side as a way to generate extra income. I will discuss the challenges or setbacks that come with building a business, as well as the great rewards. I'll also talk about the importance of developing an entrepreneur's mindset. I will walk you through a time-tested system for creating both a business and a personal budget designed to support you through the process of building your business, while exploring a great process for setting goals around your business and staying faithful to it.

I hope these stories will inspire you to work toward bringing your own dreams into reality and the creation of your own business. It is my hope that as you reach the end of this book, you're able to take many great ideas away with you.

One such story takes us back to my seventh-grade year and to the birth of a dream I've been working on ever since. The dream was for a business incubator designed to empower people to live their lives on purpose. It would empower people to take control of their surroundings, their current situations, and get them working on bringing their dreams into reality as viable businesses.

Growing up, I spent the majority of my time in a working-class environment. When I visited my father in the suburbs, I was able to experience the middle-class way of life. As young as I was, I always tried to keep an open mind and look for the good and bad parts in both worlds.

By being exposed to these two different worlds, I learned many valuable lessons about money and the mindsets behind making money. In the end, I would say the most important thing I learned is that money means choices—no more, no less. The more money a person has, the more choices he or she has. A person's values or principles will determine what choices he or she makes and what is done with the money received.

As a youngster, I often heard talk of how money corrupted people or how people with money took advantage of those without. I grew up in an area where I saw kids robbing other kids because one had something that the other wanted. I saw a guy down the street rob his neighbor so he could buy drugs. I grew up hearing phrases like, "Money is the root of all evil," but—as far as I could tell—an awful lot of evil deeds were going on around people who didn't have any money, too.

After watching people around me struggle for years, I knew there had to be a better way, and I was determined to find it. I learned early on that if your dream is big enough and if you have faith, in time you will be given the help needed to accomplish that dream. No matter how much adversity you may experience or how much you might want to give up, if you stay focused on your dream, you will have the strength to overcome any challenges.

The benefits that came with having money became very clear to me early on. The more financially endowed a person was, the more doors opened for him or her. I also realized that the amount of money people needed varied and depended on their goals and the types of lifestyles they wanted to live.

As a youngster, I also learned that—if need be—I could be completely self-sufficient. I learned how to negotiate for what I needed, and, if necessary, I could get by with just a small amount of money. I learned that when things seemed impossible, someone would show up and help make things better. I learned that sometimes I would have to push past pain, fear, and my own self-doubt, and in the end, I would became stronger for it. Most importantly, I learned it was okay to dream, because even if things didn't turn out the way I pictured, they would still be better than before.

"Give me six hours to chop down a tree, and I will spend the first four hours sharpening the axe."
— Abraham Lincoln

"We attract into our lives whatever we give our energy, focus, and attention to, whether wanted or unwanted."

— Michael J. Lasier

CHAPTER 3:
THE CORNERSTONE OF A GREAT BUSINESS

A business begins with an idea. You may have a dream, passion, or an idea for a great business concept. However, all great businesses have a few key things in common:

> ➤ A companywide mission, or an ownership mentality from the ground floor up—a mission that can live far beyond the company's founders
> ➤ An organization model designed around continued growth
> ➤ Consistent core activities
> ➤ A core business structure that is systems-based
> ➤ Short-, mid-, and long-term goals that everyone in the company can stand behind
> ➤ A solid financial foundation designed to ebb and flow around challenges

Over the years, I've had many great ideas for businesses—and any one of them may have worked if I'd only taken action. For example, when I was fifteen, I wanted to buy an old hearse and attach a powerful battery charger on the bed in the back of the vehicle. I'd go around and jumpstart people's cars when their batteries died because it was too cold. Granted, I grew up in Wisconsin, and winters were much colder then, so dying batteries were commonplace. Tow trucks would be called to homes so residents could get to work in the morning regularly.

Imagine, you wake up, shower, get dressed, and head out to work, but your car won't start. Panic arises—now what? You call for help! You look up, and what do you see? A tow truck? No! It's a shiny black hearse pulling in. Out hops a well-dressed man who opens up your hood, opens the back of the hearse, pulls out a steel bed once designed to hold a coffin, but this time, it carries a high-powered battery charger. *Voilà*! Your car quickly comes back to life. After collecting a modest fee, the gentleman drives off in the hearse and you continue on to work.

Advertising would not have been a problem for this business. People would tell that story for years to come. Stickability—that's the cornerstone for all great marketing ideas.

Then comes passion. How passionate are you about your dream or idea? Take my battery-jumping hearse, for example. Was it a good idea? Probably, but I wasn't passionate about it. Yes, I thought it was a great idea that would have been a lot of fun to do. But, quite frankly, I didn't want to go out at four o'clock in the morning in the bitter cold in order to build the business. Our passion behind an idea must equal our commitment to pursue the idea. We must have the will to bring the idea into reality, especially when an unfortunate event arises, such as

- A recession causing a decrease in the consumer's purchasing power
- Changes in regulations
- Loss of business assets
- Loss creating a large or uninsurable expense
- Loss of key employees
- Increase in manufacturing costs

The list goes on. Any one of these can wipe out a business if its foundation is not positioned to absorb the hit. That's why it's so important to build your business's foundation as you move through each stage.

If you ask me, the story of the three little pigs is one of the most profound examples of how to survive any business or financial setback. It never ceases to amaze me how many people move through life thinking all is good, even though their financial foundation or business is built like a straw house. Then, along comes a wolf, who huffs and puffs and blows their business down.

When you build your financial foundation or business inside a brick house, the wolf might break a window, but the foundation will remain strong. It is relieving to see the wolf outside and know that no matter how scary he may seem, he can't blow the door down. May this book arm you with such a foundation.

It's also very important to have a systemized marketing approach. All great marketing programs incorporate certain key components that will determine the level of efficiency and effectiveness of the program or campaign. For instance,

> They must be carried out over a predetermined period of time
> They must be relational in nature—remember, people don't care how much you know until they know how much you care
> They must be consistent—for example, a mailing that is sent out the first week of the month, each and every month, over a long period of time
> They must have a common theme, jingle, or campaign that keeps you in the forefront of your target market's mind on an ongoing basis
> They must have a systematized approach to celebrating the important dates or occasions of your clients (birthdays, anniversaries, etc.)

The trick to a well-run marketing program is to have it as automated as possible, without losing the personal touch.

The 8 Ways to Commit Entrepreneurial Suicide:

1. Trying to do it all yourself—becoming a jack of all trades and master of none.
2. Not having a business/marketing plan—getting caught up in the day-to-day tasks and not staying true to your plan.
3. Not having a solid financial plan—improperly tracking your cash flow, budget, and net worth.
4. Lack of lead generation—focusing all your energy on advertising and other forms of passive marketing instead of proactively and continually adding to your client base through referrals.

5. Running your business with a transactional focus rather than a relational focus.
6. Spending all your time working *in* your business and forgetting to work *on* your business.
7. Spending the bulk of your time working on less important activities and not focusing on the more important or core activities of the business.
8. Letting complacency set in and not continually striving to improve your skill sets, business knowledge, or growing as a person.

When you become a member of our business community, you will avoid these common pitfalls through our entrepreneurial success system. As a member of our business community, you will

➤ Be able to attend our maximum-performance training program, where you will design a systematized business plan that is designed around your "Why" or purpose for being in business, not just what you do and how you do it (along with a detailed proactive twelve-month marketing campaign tailored around meeting the needs of your ideal client)

➤ Be connected to many other professionals whose strengths are your weaknesses, allowing you to focus on the things you do best

➤ Be given a comprehensive financial plan, along with detailed business budget, net worth, cash flow, insurance, and legal reviews

➤ Have access to our comprehensive, relational marketing system designed to help you turn your clients into walking, talking advocates for your business

➤ Be shown how to build, sort, and qualify your database, allowing you to build rock-solid business relationships with your clients or customers by becoming a connector or a trusted resource for them (this is where true enterprise value is built from)

> ➢ Have access to a compressive administrative team designed to help you with all your core business tasks so you can focus on the most important activities necessary to serve your clients/customers and grow your business
> ➢ Have access to a comprehensive personal and business-development system

As you continue to read this book, I will share with you many great tools and ideas for starting, growing, and taking your business to the next level. And as a fellow alumni of this course, I would like to invite you to join our community. If you are ready to soar to great heights, then say "YES!" and send us an email: community@mycentsiblesolutions.com.

All businesses first start with a dream, vision, and well-laid plan.

CHAPTER 4:
THE BIRTH OF A DREAM

When I was in seventh grade, John, my stepfather, was the head chef at Marquette University in Milwaukee, Wisconsin. I would often go there and help him in the kitchen. Throughout the day, I listened to student workers talk about the different business and law classes they were taking. Over time, I became more and more interested in business and finances.

When John didn't need my help, I sat in on different business classes and workshops offered by the Small Business Administration. I was like a sponge, learning everything I could about business and finances, and swore that I would not grow up worrying about money like those around me did.

In these classes, I recalled stories I heard about my grandparents; they had a wig shop that ended up going out of business. I listened to the teachers in the SBA classes and wondered if, with the proper help, my grandparents might have been able to save their enterprise. I looked at different small businesses around me, and they seemed to always be trying to do everything themselves. They were working very hard, yet, one after another, they were failing. I kept thinking, *if there was a resource to help those struggling businesses, many of them may not have failed.*

Over the next few years, I took all that I learned at Marquette and created a business plan for an enterprise. It was designed to become a leader or a cornerstone between small-business owners and the core solutions needed to take their business to the next level. It was an organization designed as a safe, supportive environment for them to grow their businesses in.

When we set out to build a business, no matter how hard the challenges are, if our goals and dreams are clear and we don't let life derail us, anything is possible. True victory is shown by the winning championship; however, it is earned through all the blood, sweat, and tears that led up to the championship. Stay true to your dreams and business vision and anything is possible—if not by you, then through you.

Money and finances are the lifeblood of a business, so when we set out to build a successful business, we need to make sure we have a healthy mindset around them.

I'll never forget the time when my daughter Sabrina was in third grade. One day, she came home from school and seemed troubled. I asked her what was wrong, and she told me she'd watched one of her friends take a bunch of change out of her pocket and use it to by candy at lunch.

I asked her if she felt that her friend shouldn't have bought the candy.

Sabrina responded, "No, it's not that I don't think she should have bought the candy. What bothers me is that the change clearly didn't have any value to her. It's not like she took a handful of change out of her pocket, chose a few coins to buy the candy, then put the rest back into her pocket. She took all the change out of her pocket and gave it all to the sales lady as if it wasn't worth anything."

Sabrina then told me that she had started thinking about stories I'd told about my clients, and she began to think that if we didn't teach kids the value of money and how to properly manage it, they would end up broke and in financial trouble. I asked Sabrina what she wanted to do to help ensure that didn't happen. She said that she wanted to create a company designed around helping kids and their parents become financially literate and acquire the financial habits and disciplines needed to become financial independent. Thus, Children and Beyond was born.

Sabrina has since taught many kids money-management skills so they can grow up and not have to worry about finances. Sabrina's company teaches kids and their parents' money-management habits and offers workshops with the hope of empowering them.

Some of my own money lessons came from many years of listening to my family talk about money and politics. I learned some things from my stepfather, other lessons from living with my dad, and even more by starting different businesses as a kid.

Working at restaurants and a lot of other jobs taught me many lessons, too.

As a consultant, I have worked with clients from all different walks of life. In many cases, while some appear to be "well off," in reality they are just scrambling to "keep up with the Joneses." Unfortunately, the Joneses are broke. Joe Niego, a sales trainer I know, often says, "People spend money they don't have to buy things they don't need to impress people they don't know." If you ask me, that's a goofy way to live. Or, as I often say: "Money without sound values becomes impotent."

Instead, why not live within your means? Why not enjoy an affordable life so that later you can have everything you want? You can also help others get what they want at the same time. I have continued to study money, finances, business, and psychology. I have interviewed many different types of people and asked them what helped them become successful. Ultimately, it came down to a few basic things.

Success is the result of a properly laid plan created from a few basic principles practiced every day over an extended period of time. Success is a group activity. Very few people become successful on their own. I have found that most successful people relate that they became successful through the help of others. True business success or financial independence is a journey, and I believe it's a journey well worth taking.

As Jim Rohn has often said, "You should make it a goal to become a millionaire, not just for what you will achieve by becoming a millionaire, but rather for what it will make of you to become one." I think that applies to starting and growing a business, as well.

Success is the result of a properly laid plan created from a few basic principles practiced every day over an extended period of time.

CHAPTER 5:
A DREAM ISN'T ALWAYS A PLAN

It was 1999, and it was finished. I sat there as this amazing sense of accomplishment came over me. I looked around my office, over the desk, and to the lobby. I then scanned the receptionist's desk, a small tree, and a table with magazines on it by the large picture window that overlooked the courtyard.

I remembered back to when I was in Taiwan and the first time I walked into the office of my student named Mr. Lee. His office was very nice, and as I sat across from him, I couldn't help thinking to myself, *Someday, I'm going to have an office just like this.* Later that day, after leaving Mr. Lee's office, I had sat down and drawn a picture of my dream office. It'd had one large room with multiple desks, an inviting lobby, and a big training room for classes and seminars.

After reflecting on Mr. Lee, I got up and walked past the fully equipped supply room and into the training room. There I stood in front of a large four-by-eight-foot whiteboard and five rows of tables and chairs. My dream office had become reality. I'd done it!

As I stood there, my excitement turned into fear and then despair. Yes, my dream was real...but I had been so focused on my dream office that I'd built the office before I even had a viable business to run within it. I looked out at the Ford car dealership next door, realizing how silly it would be for Ford to build a car before they invented the engine—and then to put the car out in the lot for the world to see. Yet, that is what I had just done.

Well, technically, I had three businesses at the time. I had a limousine company, a real estate office, and a chauffeur training school. I figured I'd recruit a bunch of real estate agents, or run some ads to fill a class of students who wanted to become chauffeurs (and then work for me). Problem solved! At least, that was my thought. That was the beginning of a series of somewhat painful—but mostly expensive—lessons.

To begin with, I'm going to take you back to 1997. It had been two years since my first daughter was born and I had decided to quit my job as the general manager of a local real estate office. I'd then purchased a used six-passenger limousine and opened my limousine company so that Jennifer, my wife, could continue working at a job she'd fought really hard to get. And I could even stay at home and take care of my daughter while growing the limousine company.

I was learning a ton and beginning to make a little bit of money. However, I was getting a lot of flak from family members; they thought I should get a "real job" so Jennifer could stay home and take care of our daughter Sabrina. In reality, Jennifer loved her job, and she was making more money than I was. So, instead of staying true to my business plan, I decided I would quickly grow the company and look like a success—and family would get off my back. I then went out and bought two brand new ten-passenger limousines.

First lesson learned: *Never make emotional business decisions.* I had one other chauffeur and was just getting by with one car. Now I had to go out and drum up enough business for three cars and hire more chauffeurs.

Second lesson learned: *When your business grows by 40%, you need to redesign the current infrastructure or foundation of your business.* In two months, I tripled my fleet without improving the infrastructure or changing the way I was doing business. I just worked harder to find more clients. Jennifer would tell me that we had the most expensive landscape in the neighborhood...one tree, a couple of rosebushes, some other flowers, and three beautiful metal statues worth $200,000.

It was a rare day when all three limousines were out at the same time. I knew I had to make the phone ring. So, like most entrepreneurs, I thought more advertising was the magic answer. How do other limousine companies advertise? The Yellow Pages! I started with a small, modest ad...and quickly expanded to full-color, quarter-and-a-half-page ads in three of the largest phonebooks. I was spending $5,000 a month on Yellow Page advertising.

I figured, hey, the bigger the better, right? *Wrong!* Wrong, regardless of the fact that I then started averaging well over 100 incoming calls a day and usually booked about 10% of them.

I then hired a full time dispatcher and added three more cars to the fleet—blowing up my current foundation once again...and it drove profit even farther into the ground.

Third lesson learned: *Stay true to your plan. Don't get caught up in the process.* True growth takes time, and just because something increases revenue doesn't mean profit will follow.

For that amount of advertising, I should've had a solid client base, between ten to fifteen limousines, four to five dispatchers (not just myself and one other), and around a couple dozen chauffeurs. Had I sat down and carefully planned out the process of where I wanted to take the company...had I done the math and seen what it would've taken to support my goal, I would have seen trouble. But, like many young entrepreneurs, I ran full-steam toward my goal, trying to figure out each next move as I went along.

Because that current infrastructure couldn't handle the increase in my business, I had to "farm out" (give away) runs to other companies. As it turned out, other limousine companies had the same dilemma, so we decided to form a limousine association. We met once a month to discuss ways to improve each other's businesses and the industry as a whole.

We decide that instead of farming out a run, we would book the run and then have another company execute it as if they were part of our company. We would retain the client and they would pay us a 20% referral fee for giving them the work. Life was good, there was plenty of work to go around.

After seeing a need for trained chauffeurs, a couple of experienced chauffeurs from one of the limousine companies decided to open a chauffeur's school and acquired a really good training program. There then was an influx of trained chauffeurs in the market place. I decide to, once again, increase the fleet, and I added another limousine and a town car to the mix. This time, I redesigned the company's infrastructure to allow for the changes and just kept plugging away.

1997 was coming to an end, and Jennifer and I were gifted with beautiful twins. I was taking care of Sabrina, then two-and-a-half, and three-month-old twins. Jennifer had been promoted at her computer company job downtown, and the limousine company was rapidly growing. By the end of 1998, after setting a goal to make $100,000 in revenue that year, I finished with $200,000. Things appeared to be moving along just as planned.

In the beginning of 1999, the owners of the chauffeur's school decided to sell the school, so I agreed to buy it. I was given the opportunity to lease an office space in downtown Bellevue near Jennifer's work. I figured I would move the school to my office and continue to train people there. I would get paid to train my own chauffeurs and could hire the best students in of the classes. It seemed like a plan laced in gold.

I was in heaven until I acquired the school...and found out all the training material was copyrighted, and I didn't have permission to use the material unless I paid 40% of the revenue back to the copyright holder. It was a price I couldn't afford to pay.

Fourth lesson learned: *The true value of a business is in its current clientele and the intellectual property held by the business...NOT all of its pretty furniture.*

But, since I then had all the furniture, what better time to open my real estate office? I opened a real estate office and hoped to hire between five and ten agents.

Like many business owners caught up in the hustle and bustle, big promises, and soon-to-come fortune, I never "looked under the hood."

Fifth lesson learned: *Don't get so caught up in the outcome that you miss the process necessary to create that desired outcome...and just because a business looks great in its current form doesn't mean it will still work if it's uprooted or changed.*

On the surface, it looked like the perfect plan. The limousine company appeared to be making good money, the chauffeur school appeared to be successful in its location, and if I could hire enough agents, that would bring in an additional source of revenue. Individually, all three businesses showed great possibility. But, when they were combined together, it radically changed the chemistry and foundational integrity of each business.

On top of taking care of three small children, running a limousine company, and trying to figure out what to do with a curriculum-less chauffeur school, I was now going to build a real estate business. After all, who needs to sleep, right? And I could eat while I was driving, so that part was covered. I was not following that old saying, "Stop and smell the roses," or in my case: "Stop and smell your business." Unfortunately, my business had an ever-growing smell of manure.

Sixth lesson learned: *In business, just because it seems (and even looks) like a great idea doesn't mean it is.*

I thought I was aggressively growing my business, but subconsciously, I was piecing together my dream office. As awesome as it was once the dream became real, the office was without the necessary foundation to support itself for the long haul.

That's why it's so important to first create a detailed business plan and then a foundation strong enough to support that plan— and stay true to it. Sure, I was able to bring my dream into reality, but I did so at a much larger cost than was necessary.

When you sit down and examine your business idea or plan, there are a few key questions you need to ask.

- What are the underlying features needed for the success of the business?
- What are the core components needed for creating a solid foundation?
- What is the overall objective of the business?

Did I sit down and ask myself these questions in regard to my businesses? Did I closely analyze all that would go into growing each business? How much it would cost each one to run every month? The types of employees would I need to hire? The types of contracts I would need to acquire the businesses? Where the best locations for those types of businesses were? No! Like many aspiring entrepreneurs, I had a dream, saw what appeared to be great opportunities present themselves right in front of me, and ran full-speed ahead, never once looking back, or even sideways, for that matter.

And there I stood, in my dream office, thinking about how cool it all was. The beginning of my "empire" was about to take off. I was the proud owner of a limousine company with a fleet of seven cars, three of which were brand new limousines. I had the newest real estate office on the block! Well, the *only* real estate office on the block, or in the neighborhood, in fact...which should have been a clue. And yes, my very own chauffeur school.

Now, let me repaint the picture for you. Because I leased an office in an office park according to my dream office standards, I didn't take into consideration that I couldn't park the limousines there overnight. I still had to house the company out of my home. I was still doing about 40% of the limousine runs myself, washing and detailing the limousines myself, and was working around sixty hours a week.

I didn't have a broker who could watch over the real estate office or train and recruit new agents...which meant I had to. I also didn't have any experienced agents with great track records. So, I had to somehow find our clients—starting with the first one. That was a challenge when I wasn't in the real estate business full-time. Oh, and I had bought a school, but had no way to pay copyright fees on its curriculum because I hadn't asked for a purchasing contract. And, you guessed it: I was also the marketing person, receptionist, course creator, and head instructor for said school. Oh, and let's not forget that I was also the primary caregiver for a four-year-old and two-year-old twins. Terrible twos, you say? I wouldn't know. I was too busy to notice.

Seventh lesson learned: *When purchasing a business, an asset is only as good as its key players and the legal integrity or intellectual/contractual rights that come with the sale. Just because it looks good on the surface doesn't mean there aren't cobwebs underneath.*

"Just hire people to help!" you say. Yeah, that was my plan, too...until the phone rang, and it was the leasing company calling to inform me that two of the limousines were in default. If I didn't pay by the end of that week, they were going to repossess the limousines. Then the bank informed me that our line of credit was maxed out. How could that be? I still had checks left in the checkbook. Seriously, when I later suggest that you get both a working budget for your personal expenses as well as for your business, please, please, *please* pay attention to the system that I am going to teach you.

While wiping away tears, I walked out of the training room and back to my desk to a six-pack of beer I'd bought earlier that day. I cracked one open and sat there drinking it while I thought about all the different lessons I had learned that week.

1. *Never make emotional business decisions.*

2. *When your business grows by 40%, you need to redesign the current infrastructure or foundation of your business.*

3. *Stay true to your plan. Don't get caught up in the process.*

4. *The true value of a business is in its current clientele and the intellectual property held by the business...NOT all its pretty furniture.*

5. *Don't get so caught up in the outcome that you miss the process necessary to create that desired outcome...and just because a business looks great in its current form doesn't mean it will still work if it's uprooted or changed.*

6. *In business, just because it seems (and even looks) like a great idea doesn't mean it is.*

7. *When purchasing a business, an asset is only as good as its key players and the legal integrity or intellectual/contractual rights that come with the sale. Just because it looks good on the surface doesn't mean there aren't cobwebs underneath.*

And, finally, eighth lesson learned:

8. *While it's important to dream big, always keep your dreams in perspective with your current situation. Dreams are meant to be developed over time with the help of others. Don't try to do it all yourself. The biggest dream-killer is the power of one!*

The next day I rented a truck, went back to my office, packed everything up, and moved it all to my garage where it sat, waiting to be unpacked and brought back to life. Unfortunately, that day never came.

"Nothing can add more power to your life than concentrating all your energies on a limited set of targets."

— Nido Qubein

"I alone cannot change the world, but I can cast a stone across the waters to create many ripples"

– Mother Theresa

CHAPTER 6:
CHANGE IS THE ONLY CONSTANT

If you believe a big change is on its way, always make sure that your foundation is soundly in place and you're ready. I'm a firm believer that the more prepared you are, the fewer chances there are that something will go wrong. I think Brain Tracy coined it well when he said, "Luck is when opportunity meets preparation." Proper preparation is always the best defense. It amazes me how many people ignore the signs until it's too late. Then, when something goes wrong, they have to scramble to catch up.

When I was a kid, we had a poster on the wall in our classroom with Murphy's Law on it. As I sat at my desk, I would read, "Anything that can go wrong will go wrong," thinking about how morbid it sounded. Yet, many people seem to live by those words, or the "glass is half empty" perspective. If you ask me, the glass's fullness (or lack thereof) ultimately depends on the person filling it. I often joke around and say that if you invite Murphy, he won't show up. Or, in other words: be prepared!

I tell the people that I work with that the only constant in business is change. Preplanning for that change in order to stay on track for the desired outcome is an absolute necessity. *Who Moved My Cheese?* by Spenser Johnson not only addresses preplanning, but it's also a great bedtime story to read to your kids. Talk about planting ideas with your children. You will be amazed by some of the things they say. I know I have been.

The more people get used to dealing with change the easier it will be for them to adapt when it happens. Granted, when you are building your business, consistency is essential for developing a strong foundation. However, as things begin to change, turn those changes into teachable moments and explore their pros and cons—and even what caused those changes to happen in the first place.

Probably one of the biggest strengths I developed as a child was learning to adapt to change, because it felt like my life was changing continuously. The great part was that I often found, after the change, even better things would arise. As long as I stayed focused on the goal or end result, change was often just one door shutting and another opening. When my children were six and nine, my family's move from Seattle to Milwaukee was an important personal step in the implementation of my dream. Yet, for Jennifer, it felt like she was starting all over. And even though she had often said that she wanted to quit her job, she still loved it.

After a week or two of planning, Jennifer got her boss to let her keep her job and work remotely from Wisconsin, since most of what she did was internet-based.

On July 5th, 2005, we pulled up in front of our new house. Over the next couple of months, we settled in, and I started working as the director of training for RE/MAX. Jennifer would go upstairs to her office and work. Yet, something told me she needed to have a back-up plan, so I created a shell of a business for her—just in case the opportunity would arrive for her to break glass and bring the business to life. On November 16th, 2007, at 4:15 PM, I walked in our front door. Sabrina, who was sitting on the couch with her homework, greeted me with, "Dad, Mom just got fired. I think you'd better go see if she's all right."

When I walked into Jennifer's office, she was just staring at her desk in shock. "My boss just called. He said he was taking the business in another direction and that I would not be part of that. He then told me he had just disconnected all network connections to my computer, so I need not bother finishing out the day."

My first thought was that her boss hadn't thought this through and he needed Jennifer much more than she needed him. I asked her what she wanted to do.

"I don't know, Mike. I really like what I'm doing. I like selling computers and working with colleges on their hardware and software needs. And I really like my clients. We have built up great friendships over the years."

I then suggested that she call her customers and tell them she had been let go—and how much she had enjoyed working with them, as well.

An hour or so later, Jennifer emerged from her office with a broad smile on her face. She told me that many of her customers had not liked the company she had worked for, and that if she were to work for another company, they would follow her.

"But I don't know anyone here; how will I get a job with another computer company?"

"Maybe it's time to open your own company," I replied.

"It's not that easy," she objected.

"Just for fun, if you were to open a company, what would you call it?"

After thinking for a while, Jennifer said, "I don't know...I kinda like JR Microsystems."

I went back downstairs, turned on my computer, and completed the online paperwork to set up Jennifer's LLC. I then told her that on Monday, she would call all her customers and tell them she was now working for JR Microsystems, LLC, as the newly appointed president. She would grow the company with the help of their referrals.

She followed my recommendations, and that Monday, she learned how much her customers believed in her and her new business. Her business has grown 30% every year since then, without any changes made to her day-to-day activities. The crazy part was the company that fired her went out of business six months after letting her go.

Because we followed the plan set forth in this book and had an emergency fund, we could cover our living expenses for a year without having to tap into our investment accounts. Between what I was making and some savings, we were able to cover our family's expenses. Jennifer was able to grow her business over the course of the next year without having to take any money out of it.

Change will certainly happen, but if you plan for it, everything will work out in the end. Change isn't the enemy—it's how you respond to it that matters.

CHAPTER 7:
DEVELOPING AN ENTREPRENEUR'S MINDSET

Your income will only grow to the level of your own self-esteem.

One of the biggest challenges that entrepreneurs face when entering into business is when their past habits, beliefs, or personal philosophies follow them in their businesses. Even though these habits, skill sets, and beliefs can sometimes be great assets to a business, they can often be very limiting.

When compounded with the fact that they may not have a lot of business knowledge or experience, budding entrepreneurs can often be primed for failure from the start. Just because someone is very good at something or has a next-big-thing idea doesn't mean he or she should jump into business. There is a learning curve that an entrepreneur has to experience. It's far better to start this process at the beginning before one has a lot of time, money, and energy invested into a new business.

Now, granted, you can always hire a consultant to come to the rescue later. But, as the saying goes, "When a person with money meets a person with experience, often the person with the experience will leave with the money, and the person with the money will leave with the experience." I have done this dance many times throughout building my own businesses. Even though I walked away with many great lessons learned, my bank account suffered. It is partly due to this that I wrote this book.

Learning the lessons in this chapter has easily cost me more than a million dollars over the course of my developing a healthy entrepreneur's mindset. I hope you pay close attention to the ideas, stories, and concepts covered throughout this chapter.

A mentor once told me, "You should become a millionaire for what it will make of you to become one. It's the journey from which the greatest benefits will come."

I took those words to heart, even though making a million dollars seemed like a large task—if not an impossible one—at the time. I had three failing businesses, a $100,000 line of credit that was totally maxed out, and $80,000 in short-term credit card debt. In addition, two of our newer limousines were in default, and the bank had just told me that they were going to come and repossess them by the end of the week...and I had a family to support.

Yes, making a million dollars seemed like a great idea. However, at the time, I would have settled with getting my two limousines out of default before the bank's tow trucks showed up.

To make things worse, my three businesses had combined monthly expenses of $15,000 and monthly revenues of $8,000. On the home front, $7,500 a month was going out in personal expenses, with only $4,500 of stable income coming into cover those expenses.

I was so far off-track that I thought my working capital was the available line of credit on my credit cards. Needless to say, the concept of making a million dollars, no matter how exciting it sounded, seemed close to impossible. My goal at that time was to make $100,000—and I didn't even know how I was going to accomplish that. Now my mentor was suggesting that I set a goal to make a million dollars. Sure, it was a great idea, but let's get real. Me, make a million dollars? But on the other hand...why not me?

When I was a child, my friends and I played The Game of Life. We excitedly tried to get to the millionaire's mansion rather than land in "the poor house." The more we played the game, the easier it became to get to the millionaire's mansion. I wish someone would have told me that real life worked the same way. I would have been as careful with how I reacted to the real-life Chance Cards as I was when I played the game. I now realize that the better we get at addressing and reacting to life's lessons the easier it is to get to the millionaire's mansion.

One day, while pondering my difficult financial situation, I had the opportunity to pick up a very wealthy businessman named Mr. Chen at the Seattle Airport and drive him to

Vancouver, BC, where he was going to purchase a $200 million office building. On the way to Vancouver, we talked about business, and I asked him about the greatest lesson he had learned throughout his years and successes.

After thinking for a few moments, he said, "Get used to dealing with the problems or obstacles in business while the zeros are still small. The problems seldom change—just the zeros behind the problems or obstacles change. If you get used to dealing with the problems while they are still small, as your business or financial life grows, you won't get bogged down when challenges arise."

I didn't fully understand what he was saying until a few years later. I'd made a payroll mistake that cost me $43 and complained about it to my wife over breakfast. Later that day, I was driving the vice president of the MGM Casino to a dinner party. He was on the phone with the CFO of the casino, mad and complaining about the same things I had complained to my wife about earlier...only his was a $43,000 mistake! In a flash, I understood what Mr. Chen had meant a few years back, and my little $43 dollar mistake didn't seem so bad.

As in The Game of Life, things happen. How we react to these challenges often dictates how things will turn out. When we play The Game of Life and lose, we just pack up the game and put it back on the shelf for another day. In real life, when people lose the money game, they often pack up their dreams, goals, and empty promises and put them away...however, unlike The Game of Life, there may not be another chance to play.

I was told by different mentors that my income would only grow to the level of my own self-esteem. While that made sense on the surface, it took some time before the words really started to resonate with me. I became vigilant about what messages I was telling myself and passing down to my children.

As entrepreneurs, if we truly want to become wealthy and build a great business, we need to adopt the proper mindsets. I had a strong desire to gain wealth because I knew it would help me do many of the things I wanted to do in life. Yet, it seemed the harder I tried to gain wealth, the faster I was pushing it away.

On the surface, I wanted to attract and achieve wealth. However, from lessons I learned as a child, I believed deep down that if I acquired wealth, it would make me a bad person and I would lose the respect of those around me. I had often been told that in order to get wealthy, one had to hurt or cheat other people.

On one hand, I loved business and finances and knew I could do well and make a lot of money. On the other hand, my subconscious mind would fight me every step of the way. Initially, I thought that I wasn't very lucky or that I didn't know enough. So, I kept trying to learn more, hoping that I would find the missing link. The problem was that I was looking outside of myself for the answer, when—in fact—the answer had been buried inside of me the whole time.

My daughter Sabrina has a completely different outlook on creating wealth. She grew up learning that money or wealth is available to everyone, especially when people stay disciplined and follow the daily habits needed for acquiring wealth. As a child, she discovered that money is a tool (no more, no less) for helping us bring our goals into realty. For one person, that goal may be to put food on the table. For another, it might be taking an exciting vacation. For yet another, that goal might be to build a large business or enterprise. No one goal is better or worse than another. Every goal is important to its holder.

You may be wondering why I am discussing self-esteem and belief systems in a book about building a successful company. The answer is quite simple: If you're not careful about your own beliefs about money and wealth, your subconscious mind will continually sabotage your efforts, and it will be extremely hard to build a great business—let alone acquire wealth. The two go hand-in-hand.

Many people share the same fears or concerns about money and finances. I have found that before creating a business or financial plan, it's first necessary to help entrepreneurs work through their own beliefs about money and becoming wealthy.

Below is a list of some of the common beliefs I've seen clients struggle with:

- *Most rich people probably did something bad, dishonest, or took advantage of people to acquire their wealth.*
- *It's more righteous to be poor than to acquire wealth.*
- *Acquiring wealth takes too much work or struggle.*
- *I don't feel good or lucky enough to acquire wealth.*
- *Trying to acquire wealth won't allow much time for anything else in life.*
- *If I acquire wealth, there are certain people in my life who won't like me.*
- *Having a lot of money means you must be greedy.*
- *I don't know enough to acquire wealth.*
- *If I acquire wealth, I might lose it.*
- *If I really strive for wealth and don't succeed, I'll feel like a failure.*
- *You can't strive for wealth and be happy at the same time.*
- *It's not right to make more money than my parents.*
- *It takes money to make money.*
- *Striving for wealth can cause stress and health problems.*
- *Given my past, it would be difficult to acquire wealth.*
- *I'm too young or old to acquire wealth.*
- *I don't have the time to manage money; I don't enjoy managing money.*
- *I don't have enough money to worry about it.*
- *Financial security comes from having a good job and steady paycheck.*

Read through this list and see which messages about money you might be carrying around with you.

A strong mental foundation regarding money and wealth is what I refer to as an "entrepreneur's mindset." A large part of becoming financially independent is first developing the   proper attitude. Our financial beliefs come from a combination of our background, the people we associate with, and what we have learned about money as children and adults.

These beliefs can be very personal and, if not properly managed, very dangerous to our financial wellbeing. "Money" is mentioned more than any other word in the Bible—even "love." That leads me to believe that money is pretty important and has been for a very long time. I think that, if used wisely, money can become a blessing to many people...but if used unwisely, it can be a time bomb waiting to go off.

In American culture, we often try to lump people into various groups according to their money and finances, such as the "rich and famous" or the "poor and mistreated." If you observe the media, you'll see that it seems to either idolize wealth or look down on it. There are television shows geared toward winning millions, and others aimed at tearing apart those who have millions!

There are also many common expressions around the pursuit of money and wealth, such as, "It takes money to make money." There are many ads that "promote" money, like, "No interest until June, 2020," or, "No Credit? No problem! We love credit challenges"...sure, at 25% interest!

See if you can fill in the blanks here. "Money is the root of all _____," or, "It's easier for a camel to fit through the eye of a needle than a rich man to get into _____."

Some people have a deep-seated belief that if they made a lot of money, something bad will happen. I often hear clients say things like, "If I make a lot of money, I might lose it," or, "What will my friends and family think if I make more money than them?"

Many obstacles stand in the way of our making money, but I think fear is one of the largest ones, for it prevents us from taking action. The mind's primary job is survival, so it will try to protect us, even if it's actually hurting us or holding us captive in our comfort zones. Our financial comfort zones are in direct proportion to our beliefs about money. So, when it comes to overcoming fear, it's important to focus on our goals and what we are trying to achieve. Try to see fear as a great motivator.

I think Mark Twain coined fear well when he said, "I have been afraid of many horrible things happening in my life, some of which actually came true." At the end of the day, fear is what we make of it. The late, great motivational speaker Zig Ziglar used to use an acronym for fear: **F**alse **E**vidence **A**ppearing **R**eal!

It isn't necessary to rid yourself of fear to succeed—it's just important to learn how to make fear work for you. One key is learning how to act in spite of fear; this skill can only be mastered through practice.

The first step toward moving out of fear and into success is knowing what it is that you want and then making the decision to go out and get it. After that, train your mindset to be able to receive. As you practice these three steps, you will start to see wealth come your way.

Self-doubt will be a challenge for you throughout this process. For example, I had a client who was incredibly afraid of running out of money (regardless of his large amount of assets). One day, he just gotten out of chemo therapy. He looked like he'd been through a fight. I brought up an offer for the sale of one of his rental properties that was $10,000 less than what he was asking. He didn't want to yield and accept, even though he had plenty of equity in the property and it was a really clean offer. I told him that the buyers really wanted to buy the house, but they didn't have enough money to go any higher.

I told him the house was causing a lot of stress in his life and he really needed to focus on getting better. Yet, he asked me, "How could you be so cruel to push a sick man into a sale?" I told him, "I care about your wellbeing and the difference in the price won't make an impact in your finances. But continuing to own the house could negatively impact your health." Even though he was mad, he accepted the offer. We both learned a lesson that day.

Remember this: the difference between "poor" and "broke" is that broke is a state of your bank account, whereas poor is a state of mind. There are many people with large bank accounts who feel poor mentally. I also happen to know a lot of people who have very little money yet carry with them the influence of the rich. If we don't develop the discipline of happiness and success while we are still building our wealth, we probably won't have happiness and the feeling of success later, either. When you begin to develop an entrepreneur's mindset, it's important that you continue to re-access your beliefs and make sure that they match up with your goals.

Everyone defines financial independence differently. Some people might need $10 million before they would say they are "financially free." For others, that freedom point might be one million dollars. One of my favorite definitions of financial independence is that "financial independence is when your passive income pays for your desired standard of living or lifestyle." We all have different goals and desires, so we need to continually take a personal inventory of our values and the lifestyles we want to live. We can then build a financial foundation that will support it.

Some time ago, I learned about a great process for helping a person narrow down his or her passions about money from Values-*Based Financial Planning* by Bill Bacharch. Now, when I sit down with clients, I generally start by asking, "What's important to you about money?" When they reply, I'll follow up with, "What is it about (their answer) that's important to you?" I continue asking them about the importance of their answers until we find their core values or passions. It is at this point we can help them build a financial plan that will capture their inner goals and dreams.

An acronym I use to help clients stay focused on their financial plan is P.E.A.C.E., for financial peace comes from having control over finances. Those letters stand for **P**assionate, **E**nergized, **A**ppreciation, **C**lear, **E**mpowered. P.E.A.C.E. is then broken down like this:

- If you are **passionate** about what you are doing, the money will follow.
- Let your passion fill your spirit and keep you **energized**.
- Remember to show **appreciation** for all the people who help you along your journey.

- Keep a **clear** and concise plan for how you are going to reach your financial goals.
- Let your passion, energy, appreciative spirit, and a clear and concise financial management system **empower** you to reach even your highest goals.

Without a solid mental foundation or financial path, people tend to follow different negative patterns and repeat common mistakes, such as over-spending, making emotional (not logical) financial decisions, or avoiding an idea or action that might take them out of their comfort zones.

When a person's conscious mind is busy at work trying to figure something out, if he or she isn't careful, the subconscious mind may halt his or her actions four times harder than the conscious mind would. The ability to fully utilize a strong financial management system is empowered by how well someone is able to control the subconscious mind. The trick with financial management is to trust the system (not your internal fears) and let it do what it was created to do.

When on your computer, you may be working on one project and have another project or program working in the background. If the program running in the background suddenly developed a virus, it would most likely mess up the project you're currently working on, as well. Our brains operate in much the same way. We install virus protection software on computers to make sure this doesn't happen, yet we leave our subconscious minds exposed to all the data around us. So, when it comes to creating wealth, our financial beliefs or mindsets will generally come from the following past experiences, or "data":

Past Experiences	Present Conditions
1.) Parental influences	1.) Peer groups
2.) Our environment	2.) Financial situation
3.) Religious influences	3.) Physical well-being
4.) School days	4.) Media influences
5.) Teachers, coaches, failures	

To get around subconscious messages, we need to ask ourselves what we have learned from our pasts—the good and bad. We then need to bless our pasts for the best that has happened and forget the rest. This is very important to do so that we don't bring any negative or limiting beliefs around money or finances into our current businesses. The great thing about the subconscious mind is that it can be reprogrammed through a variety of exercises.

The three most important things for positively changing your subconscious mind are: 1) intake (for instance, the books you read or the classes you take); 2) associations (the people you spend your time with); and 3) affirmations or words and phrases you say to yourself on an ongoing basis. Let's explore these three concepts in a bit more detail.

- **Intake:** Do you like to read, listen to recordings, or attend seminars to expand your horizons and learn about how other people succeed? What kind of messages are you feeding your subconscious?
- **Associations:** Make a list of the ten people you spend most of your time with. Ask yourself: do they build me up or tear me down? If a relationship tears you down, decide which of these associations could easily be replaced.
- **Affirmations:** These are the quickest and most effective ways to change the words or phrases you use when you talk to yourself. When writing affirmations, they need to be in the present tense and affirm what is true.

Some great affirmations are:

- o I am a money magnet.
- o I prosper wherever I turn.
- o I am healthy and filled with energy.
- o I achieve the goals that I set.
- o I grow, push, and stretch.
- o I easily attract money to me.

Another great exercise is making a list of the things you've done in your life that you're proudest of. The process of writing things down and repeating them over time will make them your new reality. Over time, beliefs that become habits turn into muscle memory. Now make that list of the things you're proudest of.

- When did you feel you were at your best? That is your muscle memory.
- In what ways have you sabotaged yourself or held yourself back?

No matter what happens in someone's life, its only meaning comes from what the individual allows it. The sooner people learn this key fact, the easier it will be for them to take control of their thoughts and what they attract into their lives. When working with clients, I observe when they have thoughts or beliefs standing in the way that hold them back from reaching goals. Then I show them how they can replace those unproductive beliefs with more productive ones through the following methods.

Reframing is changing the way one evaluates the meaning of an action or situation.

Example: I once worked with a client who believed that making a lot of money was wrong because she shouldn't need that much money. She needed to see that if she made more money than she needed, she could use that additional money to help a cause that was important to her. Once she saw the benefit of making more money, how it was larger than her, she started to get excited about making more money. As her beliefs started to change, she started to find ways to attract more money into her life.

Content reframing is taking an exact situation and changing what it means.

For example, when my kids were young, I would often be out on a limousine run until two or three in the morning. So, we trained our kids to not to wake me up early in the morning.

One morning after a late-night run, I heard the twins fighting at seven AM in the kitchen, which was right above our bedroom. Seeing red, I got up and went upstairs. As I entered the kitchen, the twins looked up, saw me, and froze in their tracks.

Sam cried out, "Daddy, we are making you breakfast, and I want to make you pancakes."

Monica cried out, "But, Daddy, I want to make you French toast."

Reality set in. Yes, they were fighting, and yes, they had woken me up. But they were fighting over what to make me for breakfast. How could I be mad at them for that?

Looking at them, I said, "Kids, let's play Iron Chef. The secret ingredient is eggs. Let the contest begin!" An hour later, we had two very excited champions, and one very full dad.

Context Reframing is changing the way you see, hear, or represent a situation drastically. This means taking an experience that seems to be bad or undesirable and showing how that same behavior or experience is actually an advantage in another context. Rudolph the Red-Nosed Reindeer is a great example. While he was teased for standing out with an unusual nose, he was able to turn a potentially dismal situation around. My personal "Rudolph" experience was ending up in great debt, despite what I knew about money and finance—which made me realize that anyone can make foolish financial decisions, no matter how much they know. So, I set out to design a system to help prevent others from going through the pain I did.

Both types of reframing—content and context—alter your internal interpretations by resolving pain or conflict and therefore putting you in a more resourceful state.

Reframing is a wonderful tool when you have false or limiting beliefs. For instance, when my kids tell me they can't do something, I ask them, "You can't, or you choose not to? Either one is fine; just call it what it is." Or, if I hear them say, "I could never have or do that; it costs too much," I tell them, "It's not that it costs too much; it's that you can't currently afford it. What can you do to earn the money needed to be able to afford it?"

Now let's look at how to program your subconscious mind with positive self-talk. First, you need to reprogram your negative thoughts with positive thoughts. Here are some examples.

- "Will I ever learn how to...?" replaced with, "I learn everything I put my mind to."
- "It's another one of *those* days!" replaced with, "It's a great day; I'm ready to conquer any challenge put in front of me."

The goal is to replace negative beliefs with positive affirmations. Again, the affirmations must be in the present tense: "I exercise every day." Also, they must be specific: "I walk two miles every day." They must be personal and honest: "My health gets better and better every day." They must fit your values: "I enjoy being in good health."

If you want your affirmations to quickly take effect, you need to say them daily. You can't change your performance by focusing on where you are falling short. You must focus on what you want and act as if you have already accomplished the goal. Your subconscious mind can't tell the difference between reality and fiction.

Earl Nightingale, author of *The Strangest Secret*, would say, "What you think about, you bring about." He also was known for saying, "A person will become what he or she thinks about all day long." If people think about being happy or making money, they will achieve it. If they think about their mistakes or reasons they can't do something, they will attract that to themselves, and life will be very challenging.

Become aware of the language you use around others and your employees or customers. They won't let you down—they will become what they hear you say the most. I always cringe when I hear managers say things like, "You'll never amount to anything," and then wonder why their employees stop trying, or, "You're a slob. You never take time to..." and then wonder why their employees become inefficient.

When self-esteem is strong, you have the ability to think logically and move through any challenges. When your self-esteem is low, you tend to freeze and have trouble moving through your challenges. On another note, when pride is strong, you tend to stubbornly rely on yourself and may close yourself off from opportunities offering education or support. When your pride is hurt, you might tend to lick your mental wounds and look for outside reinforcement. This is when you are the most teachable and open to new ideas. Don't lose the teachable moments—especially with employees.

Words, when coupled with emotion, lead to powerful results. Whether good or bad, our words trigger pictures, pictures trigger emotions, and emotions trigger behavior. I remember hearing about a manager who had a sign above his desk that read, "Firings will continue until morale improves." Talk about sending a poor message. Another saying I've heard is, "In order for things to change, we have to change." If it's true that all great things must first start with an idea, then shouldn't that idea be built on a solid foundation, free of negative influence from the past? I will show you some ways to ensure that your thoughts or ideas take on a positive nature.

Some steps for changing habits and beliefs:

- **Awareness:** We need to know which habits or beliefs to change.
- **Understanding:** We need to know where the habits or beliefs came from.
- **Reconditioning:** We need to replace old habits or beliefs with new, better ones.

Our minds are more complex than any man-made machine, yet it's as simple as that computer on your desk. If you put good stuff in, then good stuff will come out. If you put bad information in, it won't run efficiently or effectively. Monitor what you say to yourself and what your employees say to themselves. Start putting more good stuff in!

If people are around unchecked negativity all the time, their self-talk will tend to be negative, as well. The importance of self-talk is also mentioned in the Bible: "As a man thinketh, so is he." Or, as Jim Rohn said in his *Achieving Excellence* series, "Don't become a victim of yourself. Forget about the thief in the alley; what about the thief in your mind?" Or, "Happiness is not an accident, nor is it something you wish for—happiness is something you design."

Truly knowing what you want is just as important as a positive mindset. People don't get what they want in life because they don't know what they want, or they spend a majority of their time thinking about what they don't have or can't do.

Clarifying what you really want in life is essential. It gives you the ability to act. It's not what you don't know that halts success—it's what you know that isn't fully developed yet. Become aware of who you are *not* and then go to work on who you are. Do you continually assess or evaluate your beliefs or habits? If your beliefs are empowering, then you need to keep them. If your beliefs are disempowering, then you need to let them go. It's very important that you continue to unlearn your old harmful beliefs and replace them with new positive ones.

A few years back, I was very frustrated with someone and was venting my thoughts while cooking dinner. After about three minutes of listening to me complain, Sabrina said, "Dad, would you agree that no one can control your emotions without your consent?"

"Yeah, why?" I said, a puzzled look on my face.

"Well, you know, Dad, you control your thoughts and your feelings, so you can either keep complaining and stay frustrated, or you can choose to think about something happy and allow your inner-happiness to come out."

My daughter was telling me to grow up. And I'd just been getting started. I was even starting to feel righteous about being angry at the person, yet that person had no clue he had even done anything wrong. Thanks to my very wise daughter, I hit the rewind button, edited out the angry thoughts, and replaced them with happy, funny thoughts. Then I pushed the play button. I disassociated from what was going on in my mind (my mental chatter) so that I could review it from a distance. It was *my choice* to hold on to my anger and frustration or replace them with more pleasant thoughts and words.

You need to reframe the past and reprogram it with the belief that will move you toward what you want. While growing your self-esteem, if you choose to neglect one aspect or belief, *that* will be the one that gets in the way.

Your beliefs are blueprints like those that provide the design for a house. Your beliefs provide the design for your future. What is your money and success blueprint? Remember, your thoughts lead to feelings, your feelings lead to actions, and your actions lead to results. You have many different blueprints. It's up to you to design your desired blueprint for success.

Another great way to develop successful habits is surrounding yourself with people who are what you want to become. This is like seeing a house and a neighborhood in which you'd like to live. You can have every investment strategy on the planet, but if you don't have the right mindset, you will probably continue to have money challenges. The true power of having a solid financial management system comes from the following equation:

Thoughts = Feelings = Actions = Results
OR
Action + Amplification = Results and Results on Top of Action = Confidence

Confidence + Momentum = A Great Attitude and a Great Attitude Brings Enthusiasm

Your income and your business will only grow as fast as your self-esteem will allow. You need to ask yourself if your current beliefs and habits will get you where you want to go. When you handle money or run your business properly, it attracts money to you. It's not the amount of money coming in that counts—it's what you do with it. In the end, money will only make you more of what you are already. To better empower you to reach great heights, here is a series of questions for you to answer.

1. Who do you know outside of your circle of influence that will help you deal with the challenges in your life? (Such as a mentor or coach.)

2. What actives will you do to help you grow this year?

3. How employable are you? (I find that once a person becomes a business-owner, it's very hard for them to go back to working for someone else.)

4. What do you need to do in order to become more confident and competent as a business-owner?

5. What changes are you willing to make in order to fulfill your life's purpose?

6. What steps are you willing to take in order to overcome complacency in your life?

7. How do you define the "next level" in your business?

8. Have you learned to be happy where you're at?

9. What changes are you willing to make in order to become a bigger thinker? (Remember, your income will only grow to the level of your self-esteem.)

10. How will you know if the changes you're making are the right ones?

11. How much money do you spend on your personal or business development?

12. Are you spending too much, too little, or not enough on your personal needs?

13. What steps are you willing to take in order to work with a good training program?

14. How do you turn yourself around when you get in a slump?

15. What systems do you have in place to pace yourself?

16. How will you learn to remove doubts about what you're doing or what you are?

17. How will you persevere through the obstacles, pitfalls, and traps that you will encounter along the way?

18. How many hours a day should you spend studying, working, etc., in order to reach your goals?

19. What types of training should you be focusing on?

20. What motivates you to remain positive on the days that you don't feel like it?

21. What is the biggest challenge you face in staying motivated?

22. What are your expectations in terms of self-improvement?

23. What do you think should be happening?

24. What is actually happening?

25. How long are you willing to wait for your personal-improvement efforts to yield results?

26. What do you think will be the biggest challenge in getting to that point?

27. How long will it take to get meaningful results if you continue to grow?

28. How do you make time to study?

29. What changes will you need to make in terms of habits and skills?

30. Will you attend workshops or meet with a personal or business coach?

31. What is the hardest challenge that you need to overcome during a normal week?

32. How will you overcome the challenge?

33. How do you handle any negative self-talk that comes up during the day?

34. What are your strengths?

35. What are your weaknesses?

36. How do you handle the following conditions?

   o   Negative thoughts

   o   Past memories

   o   Personal rejection

   o   Other people's criticism

37. How do you target specific areas in your personal-growth activities?

38. What is your biggest accomplishment, and how has it affected your life? (Even though the goal is to continually keep growing, and not focus on the past.) What accomplishments do you want to complete within the next couple of months?

39. On average, how much time do you spend on spiritual, physical, financial, business, and personal goals?

40. What is the costliest mistake or course correction you have made in the past, and why?

41. How did you learn from your past mistakes or course corrections?

42. What do you do to keep in a positive state of mind?

43. What publications or books do you read, and how often do you read them? (I have found that, at the bare minimum, you should read at least one book a month.)

44. What it the best book you read this year?

45. As you continue to grow, what kinds of responses do you get from friends or family?

46. What kind of information do you collect on personal or business growth?

47. Do you ever test your ideas before you do them?

48. What is your process for handling problems that arise?

49. Can you outline your steps for handling negative thoughts?

50. How are your positive thoughts processed?

51. How much time do you spend on a daily and weekly basis doing positive things?

52. What is your pain tolerance for dealing with tough situations?

53. What is your most productive source for getting personal- and business-growth material?

54. What one thought would you like to share with other people on how to increase their self-confidence?

55. How much effort or dedication do you put into your business- and personal-improvement areas?

56. What price have you paid in order to reach your current success?

57. And what price are you willing to pay in order to reach true success?

58. What price are you prepared to pay in order to go even farther than you are right now?

59. What has been the evolution of your life and the turning points that have accrued?

60. Where do you see yourself and your business in one, three, or five years from now?

61. What motivates you to stay focused every day?

62. When the pressures of life become overwhelming, what keeps you from giving in?

63. Are there any things that are holding you back from achieving the level or success that you deserve?

64. What are the thoughts, words, or actions that have stopped you from reaching the level you want?

    Now, let's take a look at personal affirmations. How often do you say them, if at all? Here are some questions regarding affirmations.

65. Do you say affirmations on a daily basis?

66. How many should you say every day, based on your goals?

67. How long are the affirmations?

68. How long should they be?

69. Are they memorized?

70. When saying affirmations, do you follow a written script?

71. Have you ever recorded affirmations on tape or video?

72. Do you prepare affirmations around all your goals and desired habits?

73. Do you have a time in your schedule for studying and saying affirmations?

"Everything can be taken from a man but one thing: the last of the human freedoms, to choose one's attitude in any given set of circumstances, to choose one's own way."

— Viktor Frankel

"When presented with a new idea, check your ego at the door and suspend your disbelief. Your ability to open your mind and consider new ideas without fear will propel you to the top faster than anything else."

— Bill Gov

CHAPTER 8:
BUILDING YOUR BUSINESS ON A SOLID FOUNDATION

My kids went to school to get a basic education and then came home to learn about business and finances. When they were small, I was determined to make sure they grew up learning about money and how to properly manage it. Financial management is an ongoing process, and the more we stay dedicated to our plan, the faster we will see our dreams and goals become true.

One of the largest killers of businesses is a weak financial foundation. The phrase "cash flow is king" really holds true for businesses. Cash flow is the lifeblood of any business, and if it dries up, the business will be unable to operate. Many entrepreneurs come up with a great product or service idea and want to bring it to market, yet they don't have the financial resources or knowledge needed to truly pull it off.

When sitting down with people, whether it's regarding their businesses or personal finances, I often hear them say things like, "I don't have very much money, so why do I need to worry about managing it now?" or, "I know I should pay myself first, and I will—I just need to make a little more first." Then there's my least favorite: "I don't need that much money to get by." True, but what if you had the ability to make more money than you need? How many great causes or people would you be able to help? If we can do something that would help others and we don't do it, we are not only cheating them, we are cheating ourselves, as well.

The average high school senior will have many important life skills, yet knowing how to build a business or manage money likely won't be one of them. In fact, the average high school senior can't even balance a checkbook, let alone manage money. They then go to college, and by the time they graduate, they often have hefty student loans and credit card debt. It is for these reasons that people need to learn core financial management skills before entering into business.

If blooming entrepreneurs wait until after they open their businesses to acquire these skills, it may be too late. The question is, if schools aren't teaching people about money and how to manage it, where will they learn those skills?

Many people will finish high school and college and then decide to go into business for themselves. The problem is that, just like with financial management, core business skills aren't taught, either. These skills are either acquired through trial and error (which can be very costly) or hiring someone to help them perform various day-to-day activities.

Granted, it's very important to delegate our core business activities. However, if we don't know how to prioritize these activities or who is best suited to perform them, it can also be a very expensive process. Here is a list of some of some common business expenses that people spend money on—often before there is really a need for the product or service.

- New computer equipment with the latest software: $1,000 to $2,500
- Marketing/promotional materials, business cards, flyers, tri folds, postcards, etc.: $500 to $2,500
- Direct marketing campaign: $500 to $3,000
- Website: $500 to $5,000
- Business start-up, legal/accounting fees: $500 to $2,000
- Employees: $1,000 to $25,000
- Business courses or workshops: $200 to $1,000

As you can see, these things can be very expensive if not properly managed. Society assumes that people learn this in school and then wonders why history repeats itself. I say it's time to stop that assumption and start from the ground floor up.

Entrepreneurs need to have a track to run on—a place or organization where they can get the necessary resources for growing their businesses without spending a lot of money. My goal with this book is to give you the core systems needed to build a business, then invite you to join our community of entrepreneurs and leaders posed to move businesses to the next level and beyond. In the next section, I'm going to cover the four pillars that are the cornerstone of a solid business foundation. I'm going to show you how to grow your business without spending a lot of money in the process. In Section Three, I'm going to go over a detailed process for creating both a business and personal budget and net worth statement. This will aid you in paying off any debts that you may have and ensure you have the proper protection in place to prepare for any unforeseen circumstances.

As an example, if you have kids that are past the age of eight, a great way to save on labor costs is to hire them and put them on your payroll to do odd jobs. The amount you pay them, however, needs to be standard with what you would pay an average employee for doing the same work.

When our kids were little, if they needed money for something, they would look around the house and find something that needed to be done. They would then bring me a proposal for the job with a requested compensation amount. And if it made sense, I'd hire them to do it.

Over the years, Jennifer and I have never given our kids an allowance—but we have often paid them for doing random jobs.
I personally believe this is where the true spirit of entrepreneurism comes from. Later in this book, I will share different stories with you about how making our children responsible for their own money came in handy.

Financial independence: having a pot of money large enough that the interest or passive income from it will pay for your desired lifestyle.

SECTION TWO

LEAD GENERATION

THE FOUR PILLARS BEHIND EVERY GREAT BUSINESS

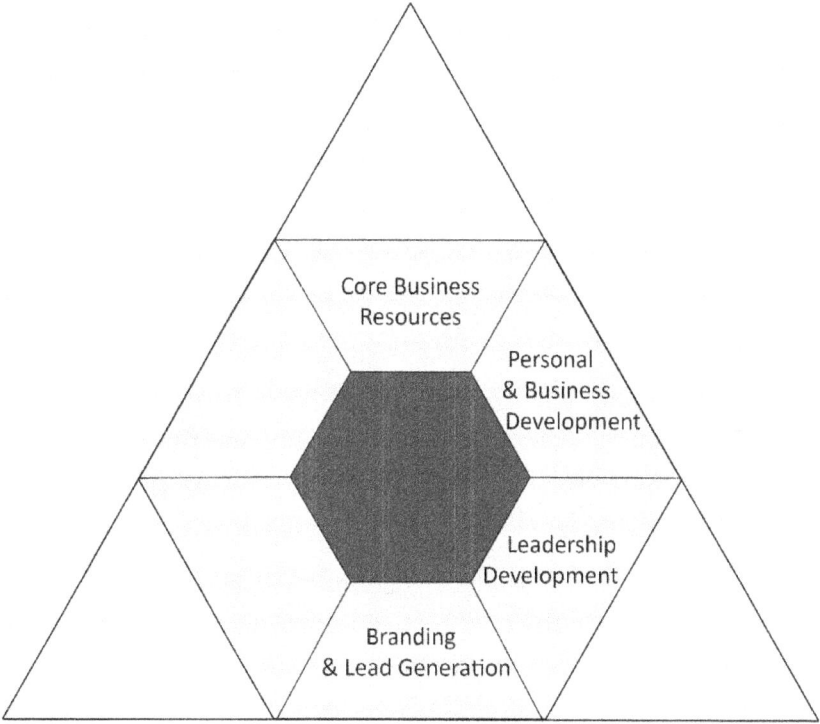

Core Business
Resources

Personal
& Business
Development

Leadership
Development

Branding
& Lead Generation

CHAPTER 9:
LEAD GENERATION

There are three main challenges with lead generation. The first and probably largest challenge I have found is the lack of priority toward lead generation in general.

When I speak with entrepreneurs, I find they spend a majority of their time on what they are in business to do. The plumber fixes toilets, the accountant crunches numbers, and the real estate agent shows houses. They also spend a good part of their time putting out fires and handling customer service and administration activities. Lead generation maybe fits in there and, if there is time left after that, some business and financial planning. Without leads or people in your calendar, you won't be able to stay in business. Lead generation is the main engine behind most businesses.

The second challenge is that people are often passive about lead generation instead of proactive. Examples of passive approaches are advertising, direct mail, or hoping for referrals (but not actively working a referral system). Proactive lead generation would be cold calling, knocking on doors, networking, or actively working a referral system.

The third challenge is most entrepreneurs aren't sure what to say when talking to a potential client or customer. Seasoned salespeople have learned to internalize scripts or dialogues when prospecting. A lot of entrepreneurs will just try to wing it. This is why this book has a section on prospecting.

I will start with the more common sales systems, such as cold calling, direct mail, traditional advertising, and networking. Cold calling is verbally contacting a potential prospect whom you have never met or communicated with. When I was in real estate, I would call through a reverse directory which listed people's names, addresses, and phone numbers. I would also call expired listings or people who were selling their houses themselves.

There are also companies that will create lists of potential leads by interest, categories, or companies. The lists can be purchased for a fee. In my experience, cold calling can be one of the hardest ways to generate leads. However, if you do it enough, you are guaranteed to get results.

There's validity to the saying, "Sales is a numbers game." If you contact enough people, even though it's a cold call, you will eventually get a qualified lead. When I was in real estate, I knew that if I called 125 people, I would land one closed transaction on average. Granted, I may've had to call a couple thousand people for the average to apply. Up there with cold calling is knocking on doors. Again, in real estate, we would select a neighborhood and knock on every door to see if people were interested in selling their houses. Another example is a friend of mine who sells websites: he will walk into many businesses in a neighborhood and see if the owner needs a website.

On the flip side, there's what is known as a warm call. This is involves a slight relationship with the person being contacted. An example is someone who is referred to you. Even though you don't know the person, there is a perceived trust between the potential client and the person who referred you to him or her—and that trust carries over to you. It could also be someone you met at a party or a networking group. You don't really know the person yet, but because you were both once at the same place, that call carries with it a little more trust. The point of a warm call is having a *reason* to call the person, not just seeing if he or she wants what you are selling.

I think most people would be far more preferable to warm calls rather than cold calls. In the next section, I will share a system with you designed to make it so all (or at least the majority) of your calls are warm calls.

Whether you are going to make cold or warm calls, it's very important that you log these calls. If you don't know your call-to-lead-to-appointment ratio, it's very hard to know if you're accurately predicting your results. There is a chart on the next page that I've used when making calls. For your convenience, you can go to www.entrepreneurshipthatmakescents.com and print out a copy, as well.

Cold/Warm Calling Numbers

Date				Cold	Calls				
1	2	3	4	5	6	7	8	9	10
11	12	13	14	15	16	17	18	19	20
21	22	23	24	25	26	27	28	29	30
31	32	33	34	35	36	37	48	39	40
41	42	43	44	45	46	47	48	49	50
51	52	53	54	55	56	57	58	59	60
61	62	63	64	65	66	67	68	69	70
71	72	73	74	75	76	77	78	79	80
81	82	83	84	85	86	87	88	89	90
91	92	93	94	95	96	97	98	99	100
100	102	103	104	105	106	107	108	109	110
111	112	113	114	115	116	117	118	119	120
121	122	123	124	125	126	127	128	129	130
131	132	133	134	135	136	137	138	139	140
141	142	143	144	145	146	147	148	149	150
151	152	153	154	155	156	157	158	159	160
161	162	163	164	165	166	167	168	169	170
171	172	173	174	175	176	177	178	179	180
181	182	183	184	185	186	187	188	189	190
Leads									
1	2	3	4	5	6	7	8	9	10
11	12	13	14	15	16	17	18	19	20
21	22	23	24	25	26	27	28	29	30
31	32	33	34	35	36	37	38	39	40
41	42	43	44	45	46	47	48	49	50
Appts.									
1	2	3	4	5	6	7	8	9	10
11	12	13	14	15	16	17	18	19	20

Another common form of prospecting is direct mail. This is very common for service-related companies. One advantage to direct mail is the ability to reach a large market-share. It's common to reach 10,000 addresses with just one mailing. The downside, though, is the average conversion rate is between 1 and 2% of the total mailing. So, you need to send out a lot of mailings in order to get a decent return. It also takes a while to receive recognition or response.

I find that entrepreneurs will send out a mailing or two and then wonder why they didn't get a decent return. It takes a while to find a good rhythm with the mailings you send out and your desired return on those mailings. You need to make a commitment to consistently send out the mailing for at least six months to a year. This is why direct mail can an expensive tactic, given the overall return on investment.

A while back, I was in a seminar discussing prospecting, and a real estate agent in the audience stood to share and share that she sent recipe cards out every month to a target market neighborhood for two years. One day, she received a call from a lady who had been receiving the recipe cards from her for those two years. The lady told her that she really enjoyed getting the cards—in fact, she had made many of the recipes. The lady then asked if the agent could please continue sending the cards to her new address.

After a short pause, the real estate agent said, "But I didn't help you sell your old house or help you buy your new one."

"Oh, no," The lady answered. "I listed my house with an agent who would send me information on market conditions and ways to prepare a house for sale, and I found my new house at an open house I attended."

You see, the lady clearly liked the recipe cards, but they didn't demonstrate the agent's competence or ability to sell a house. When it came time to sell her house, she went with the agent who seemed the most qualified...and sadly, the agent sending out recipe cards was just as good as the competing agent.

One way to get around low returns and warm up your calls is to use the mailing itself as the reason for the call. Keep in mind, though, if you're going to make follow-up calls on the mailing, don't mail out 10,000 pieces. Rather, send a mailing to as many people as you're able to call.

Let's say you are going to call twenty-five people a day. Send out one hundred pieces at a time. If you send the mailing out on Thursday and wait a few days for it to arrive, then start making your twenty-five calls on Monday. Then send out the next batch of mailings on Thursday. Customers will receive them by Monday of the upcoming week. If you repeat this process each week, you will always have people to call or follow-up with, and your calls will become warm calls. I have found that when I follow-up a mailing with a phone call, the average return is five times more than that of just a mailing.

Let's say that I mailed out a piece on the five best ways to use social media. When calling a mailing recipient, my conversation would start like this: "Hi, Mr. Peterson. This is Mike Raber, I sent you an article talking about the five best ways to use social media. Did you receive it?"

"Yes, I did," is the ideal reply.

"Great. I hope that you found it interesting."

"Yes, in fact, the part about using Facebook to find an old friend was helpful," is another ideal reply.

"Good! I'm glad you found it helpful. It has been a great tool for me in the past, so I wanted to share it with people in my community. It's my goal as a real estate professional to be a resource for others. Well, I know you're busy, Mr. Peterson, so I won't keep you. I just wanted to introduce myself and let you know that if you or anyone you care about should ever need a real estate professional, I'm here for you."

"Sounds great. Thanks for the call."

"My pleasure. And if you would like, I will send you more helpful articles from time to time."

"That sounds good."

Now I have Mr. Peterson's permission to send him more articles. If no one answers the phone and I get voicemail, I will say something like, "Hi, Mr. Peterson, this is Mike Raber. I just sent you an article on the five best ways to use social media. I hope that you found the article helpful, and I will check back with you in the near future. In the meantime, if you should have any questions, my number is on the mailing." This type of call often goes much better than just calling someone out of the blue.

Probably the most common form of lead generation is traditional advertising. We all know that companies run ads in magazines or the newspaper. However, it tends to be the most expensive form of lead generation. When I had my limousine company, I used the Yellow Pages as my main form of advertising, as you may recall. I also used direct mail, but I found it was costlier and harder to predict what my return-on-investment would be.

In business and sales, lead generation is easily one of the most important activities. Yet, as I pointed out earlier, it often gets the least an amount of attention, right up there with business and financial planning. I think that many businesses don't have the budget to pay for more traditional forms of lead generation, or they have in the past and got burned by it...or they tried cold calling and realized they didn't like rejection.

Next, I am going to explore networking. Networking is a contact sport. It takes work to turn a contact into a lead. Many people will attend a networking event in hopes of finding new business or contacts. These people will often fail to have a desired outcome before they get there—big mistake. Many people will go to an event and try to get as many cards as possible, or they may just pick out a couple of people and talk to them the entire time. In these cases, they could leave without making any actual contacts at all.

But, other people leave networking events with multiple contacts, or even set appointments. Let's say a financial advisor thinks, *I'm going to the event tonight and will meet three people between the ages of 45 and 60 that have at least $100,000 to invest.* Or, *I'm going to set three appointments with people who want me to help them prepare a financial plan.* A plumber would think, *I want to meet two realtors that will refer me to their clients.* If you know your ideal outcome, then you will know what types of questions to ask when talking with people.

The most important key to networking: ask people questions. In negotiation, there is a saying: "The person who talks first loses!" In networking, the same holds true. The next time you're at a networking event, try to learn four to seven new things about each person you speak with—specifically regarding his or her business.

When it comes to business cards, I have found there are two common mistakes people make at networking events. Some will treat their business cards like they're made of gold and hesitate to give them out. There is also the person who hands them to anyone that will take one. You will also see the individual who walks through the room and collects as many cards as possible—as if the cards themselves were business.

Whenever I go to a networking event or meeting, before I even enter the room, I think about why I'm there and what my desired outcome is. What type of client am I looking for? How many appointments do I want to make? Upon entering, I first scan the room and see if there is anyone that immediately matches the criteria for my goals. I then move around the room and ask people questions that will aid me in determining if they match those requirements.

Don't just go to events to find new leads or clients, though. Instead, find "power partners": other professionals whose businesses work well with what you do. Think of needs that people you know have, and who would best fill that need. When talking with someone at a networking event, ask yourself the following questions:

✓ Do I know anyone this person may be able to help?
✓ Does this person have a need that I can service?
✓ Would this person make a great ambassador for my business?
✓ Would this person make a good power partner?

Try to limit conversations to a few minutes. That way, if there isn't a fit, you can politely excuse yourself and move to the next person. If there is a fit, then try to set an appointment for a later time.

I will tell prospective power partners that I would really like to learn more about what they are doing—"It sounds like there may be some great ways for us to synergize. Let's set up a thirty-minute meeting for next week." I'll then invite them to my office or a coffee shop, depending on the situation. I'll then ask what their week is looking like, and book the appointment.

It's important when booking the appointment that you only give the person a few available times to meet, otherwise you'll give the impression that you're not very busy.

I will then talk to a few more people. Once I get back to the office, I'll send personal notes saying that I really enjoyed talking with them and that I look forward to learning more about what they do.

Once you're in the appointment, ask open-ended questions; spend time trying to learn as much about the other person and what they do as possible. Some examples of open-ended questions are, "How long have you been an accountant?" or, "What is your ideal client like?" There is a list of more questions in the reference section in the back of this book.

I was sitting down with a potential client and asked him what his database was like. He pulled out a stack of business cards two-inches thick. Puzzled, I asked him, "Can you tell me ten things about each of those people beside what they do?" He responded, "I don't know...I'd know a couple things, maybe." I suggested that he pick out five cards each week and invite those people to coffee so he could learn more about them.

I then suggested that he try to find a common thread between what he does and what those people do. I told him that he should always be asking if there is potential for doing business with these people...or if he could refer these people to his clients. I also suggested that he create a referral directory.

When I had my limousine business, one of my greatest tools was a referral directory. It was a list of many different businesses or service-providers that I worked with and trusted to care for my clients. When clients had needs, it was easy for me to connect them with someone who could help.

Going to networking meetings or chamber events is not just a great way to meet other entrepreneurs, businesspeople, and potential clients and costumers—it's also a great way to grow your database. When it comes to lead generation, it's very important to continually grow, sort, and qualify your database. You can then use the referral system I will cover in the next chapter to stay in touch with those in your database on a regular basis.

Continually asking your clients and customers for referrals is probably the best proactive lead-generation system. Just make sure you ask in a way that makes it a win/win— "Because I value you as a client, I'm never too busy to take care of people you care about," as opposed to, "Please give my card to people you know that need my services."

Another great way to generate leads, grow your database, and build up your referral directory is a system called a cross-endorsement program. It allows you to serve your clients at a deeper level while simultaneously prospecting for new leads.

Cross-Endorsement Program: A tool for growing your database through promoting other businesses. You reach out to another business and offer to introduce them to your clients or costumers, and in exchange, they will introduce you to their clients or customers.

For example, when I was running Newcastle Limousine, I sent a monthly mailing program letter to my clients that endorsed a CPA I worked with. I included a coupon for a free sixty-minute tax consultation. I was able to give my clients something of value, and the CPA had the opportunity to meet new clients. In exchange, he sent a letter to his clients endorsing my limousine company, including a coupon for one free hour when they rented a limousine for three or more hours. We both were able to serve our clients at a deeper level—and we both acquired new clients.

One question I'm often asked is, "What if the mailings are different sizes? My mailing list has 200 people on it, but the other mailing has 600 people." The solution is simple: you pay for the mailing that's endorsing your business and the other person pays for the mailing that is endorsing their business.

Another common concern I hear is, "But I don't want to give my database to someone else." You don't have to. I gave the letter and coupon to the CPA, and he mailed it to *his* database (and I did the same for him). We never exchanged databases. The trick is to write the letter persuasively and have a coupon with enough value that the recipient will want call you. Once they call, you can add them to your database.

"There are four ways, and only four ways, in which we have contact with the world. We are evaluated and classified by these four contacts: what we do, how we look, what we say, and how we say it."

– Dale Carnegie

"Discipline yourself to do the things you need to do when you need to do them, and the day will come when you will be able to do the things you want to do when you want to do them."

– Zig Ziglar

CHAPTER 10:
DEVELOPING A REFERRAL-BASED BUSINESS

The Referral Triangle

While running Newcastle Limousine, I knew I had to radically change the way I was attracting new clients. At the time, I was spending $5,000 a month on Yellow Pages advertising, attending networking groups ($400 a year), and paying someone $1,000 a month to answer the phones and take care of all incoming calls. Because I needed to change my approach, I analyzed other successful people and what they were doing. The one common denominator seemed to be that they had become the trusted advisor to their clients—and due to that, they would often receive multiple referrals from each of those clients.

It was at this point that I was told about The Turning Point Retreat®. As I mentioned before, Brain Buffini, the presenter, shared a system with me that drastically changed the way I did business and allowed me to become the trusted advisor to my clients I'd always wanted to be.

I spent a large amount of time meeting with and talking to different business owners and professionals. As I started to get to know them, I found what their strong points and ideal customers were. I looked for ways I could be the connection between them and my clients who needed their services.

All I needed to do was get my clients in the habit of calling me when such a need would arise. I would then facilitate the process like a concierge in a high-end hotel. I then designed a process that I called The Referral Triangle.

The Referral Triangle became a referral directory or source for both the businesses and my clients. I would often joke around and say, "Think of me as Jeeves, your personal concierge." I then made the conscious decision to start building my business by referrals instead of relying on traditional forms of advertising (like the Yellow Pages, networking, direct mail, etc.).

Over time, I became the hub between my clients and many different service providers.

If you serve your clients to the best of your ability, they will learn to look to you as a trusted advisor. They will stay loyal to you, and freely refer you to others.

When you strive to continually improve upon what you're doing and do right by your clients and customers, you will be blessed many times over. Take care of your customers and they will take care of you—it's that simple.

Mary, a client of mine, once bought a new house with a large foyer that she wanted to paint. On the way home from the airport one day, I was explaining my offering a personal concierge service to my clients. When I dropped her off at home, she mentioned her painting dilemma.

"As a matter of fact, I know a great painter," I said. "His name is John. If it's okay, I will have him call you. He's a really nice guy."

I then called John, explained the situation to him, and asked him to contact Mary. A little while later, John called back and said that he was meeting with Mary on Monday, and if all went well, he would be able to paint the foyer in one day. After his day of work was done, I called Mary to see how everything went. Mary said, "I'm surprised that you knew John had even been to my house and that you bothered to call and find out how it went."

I replied, "Of course, Mary—you are very important to me, and I don't take being your trusted advisor lightly. I'm glad I could help make this happen. How did John do?"

"He was great—very professional. I would hire him again." Mary said.

"I'm glad that John was able to serve your needs. I'm always here for you, so if you ever have anything I can help with, please let me know."

"I will, Mike, and thanks again." Mary responded.

I then called John and thanked him for taking such good care of Mary. John thanked me for the referral. I then thanked John for his professionalism and told him I would give him more referrals—and that I was never too busy for anyone he'd refer to me.

Later that week, Mary had a party and invited many of her friends. Four of those friends asked her who painted her foyer, and she recounted the story. They responded with, "Wow! And we're happy if our limousine driver just shows up on time...can he do the same for us?"

"I don't see why not," Mary replied, "It's just the way he runs his business."

The following month, I received four corporate accounts from the people who were at Mary's party. It's not always what we *do*—it's how we make our clients *feel* that makes the biggest difference. As the old saying goes, "People don't care how much we know until they know how much we care." Do your clients see you as a trusted advisor, or just another service provider? How do your clients see you? How do you set yourself apart from your competition? Once your clients no longer consider doing business with anyone but you, you will be on your way to greatness.

Competition is what you make of it—no more, no less. When you set out to truly serve your clients, you will find that competition no longer exists, and if it does, it's friendly competition.

When it comes to really building your business by referral, you need to be very proactive in your execution. It's amazing how many people will throw an ad in the paper and just sit back, waiting for a referral to magically appear. Clients are very busy—they aren't sitting around waiting for an opportunity to refer us...they need to be asked and shown how to do so. You can't just hope or assume referrals will happen.

One of my business pet peeves is hearing someone say, "I do a great job, so people should refer others to me." Being a professional, people expect you to do a great job. Just because someone does a great job doesn't mean they've fully earned a referral. It should be a natural response to how you made the client feel, and even then, only about seventy percent of the people you serve will refer you.

If you put one hundred people in a room, about thirty people will actively refer you to providers they like. About forty people will refer you to someone only if you ask them who they know. About thirty of those people aren't the referring type.

There are some people that still won't refer you, no matter how much they love your business or service. That's okay; they can still be great clients or customers. That being said, the easiest way to get multiple referrals from your clients is by following these three steps:

1. Do such a great job that the customer is so excited they tell everyone around them about the experience they had. This will cause other people to want the same experience. A great example of this is Nordstrom. Their customers are always beaming about them.

2. Build a strong relationship with your clients or customers so they feel like they are part of a community. This will draw in other people. Take Apple as an example. They have great products, but more importantly, Apple has built an entire culture that people want to be a part of.

3. Have a systemized approach to how you stay in continual contact with your clients and ask for referrals. I have found that clients have to be asked for a referral more than five times before they start referring you on a steady basis. People are very busy, and unless they see your name or hear from you on a regular basis, you won't make it past what I call their "reticular activator."

Embracing the Power of the Reticular Activator

Are you in your clients' reticular activator? And what the heck is a reticular activator? Think of it as a giant filter, like one you'd use to brew your coffee. In this case, your reticular activator filters out any unnecessary noise or outside stimuli that doesn't directly relate to what you are currently working on. It keeps you from experiencing information overload.

Think of a time you were talking to someone in a restaurant. Imagine trying to hold that conversation if every single thing around you caught your attention. If you were trying to complete a goal or project, imagine how hard it'd be to avoid getting pulled in a million directions. Imagine you have purchased a new car, and right as you pull off the lot, you start seeing the same exact car everywhere. Similarly, when my wife and I found out we were having twins, suddenly everything had something to do with twins.

If you only talk to or see your clients a few times a year, you will only be in their thoughts for a short amount of time. If this is the case, even if the opportunity arises where they could refer you, chances are the opportunity will fly right by. But if they see or talk to you frequently (and you remind them that you are never too busy for them), you will be within their reticular activator, and the referral will most likely take place.

One of the biggest challenges in getting referrals from our clients is staying in the forefront of their minds. No matter how much a client likes us or our services, as they get busy, we will start to drift into the background.

Some companies avoid this through advertising, or developing a strong brand loyalty (Apple, Band-Aid, or McDonalds). You may be saying to yourself, "How am I going to compete with companies with advertising budgets of that size?" Simple: you don't have to. You're not trying to market to the masses—just your own clients or database. That can be done through ongoing contact with said clients or database.

For my limousine business, this went hand-in-hand with my monthly mailings and follow-up phone calls. Many times I would simply leave a message saying, "Hi, Mary. This is Mike with Newcastle Limousine. I'm just giving you a quick call to say hi and make sure you got the letter I sent you. I hope you enjoyed it, and because I value you as great client, I'm never too busy for anyone you care about." Often, after the letter went out, I would get multiple referrals shortly following the mailings.

One morning, I received a call from an executive assistant I'd worked with for two years. She'd usually rented a town car to take her boss to the airport about six times a year. She started the call by saying, "Hi, Mike—this is Sally. I wanted to let you know that I'm no longer working for BF Goodrich. I just became the executive assistant to the CEO of the Seattle Macy's." She continued, "Another important CEO just flew in from New York, and the limousine they scheduled didn't show up...so he had to take a taxi from his corporate jet to our office here. He was not happy—and while he was in my office venting about it, he saw the letter you sent me. I told him about you and your business. Then he asked me, 'What does this have to do with transportation?' I explained that your business covers lots of topics for customers' personal benefits. Then he asked if you could come here and take him back to his jet."

Later that day, I picked this man up at the office and took him to his corporate jet. We discussed business, family, and my marketing system. We reached his jet and he asked me, "Do you take transportation as seriously as you take your marketing?"

"Of course," I replied. "Our marketing is what brings new clients in the door, but our transportation and customer service are what brings them back; more importantly, make them want to refer new clients to us."

"Well, you have our future business, then," he smiled. He shook my hand and got on the plane. That was the beginning of a $50,000-a-year contract.

The purpose of a monthly letter is to give clients valuable information. But most importantly, it gives you a reason to call or stop by and visit the people in your database. If your mailing contains beneficial information, they'll share it with other people and talk about you and your service or business.

The important thing to remember is that the content of the letter can't be about you or industry-specific. It needs to be relevant to your clients' lives (with an element of professionalism). I repeat: "People don't care about how much you know until they know how much you care."

There are two sides to every business transaction. One is the professional side. How good are you at what you do? When communicating with your customers, do you express that you have the necessary skills to get the job done right? It's very important that you demonstrate excellence in your services. People want to work with those who are qualified and confident.

The other side is personal. Do your clients see you as just a salesperson, or a trusted advisor? Do they know that you truly care for their well-beings? In sales, many people are more transaction-orientated. They close a sale and just move to the next one. Most people truly do mean well, but they give off the impression that they're more focused on the money.

One of my mentors, Joe Niego, once interviewed people on the streets of downtown Chicago. He asked them if they used a real estate professional to help them buy or sell their houses. If they said yes, he asked if they enjoyed the experience. Many said, "Yes, we would definitely use them again." He asked if they would refer that agent to someone. If so, he'd then ask the name of the agent. Nine times out of ten, they would respond, "Oh, wait...what was the agent's name, again?" They'd smile and admit they didn't remember.

Joe would follow up with, "If you don't remember the agent's name, how will you refer them?"

Again, they would smile and say, "Good point. I guess I couldn't refer them." Many people have great intentions and truly enjoyed a sales experience, but if the professional doesn't stay in contact with the person, no other sales can be made. Not only do you want to stay in your clients' reticular activator, you have to continually demonstrate that you are good at what you do and that you care about them.

The Business Card and The Referral

When you're building your business by referrals, the way you treat your business card will also make a huge difference. Remember my limousine business friends and our meetings? One week—right before prom season—we were gathered, and I got a call for a prom run. I was booked solid, and to the best of my knowledge, so was everyone else...except Darwin, another limo company owner. He was sitting across from me. I told the person on the phone that I knew someone who could help. I gave the person Darwin's phone number.

Fifteen minutes later, the person still hadn't called Darwin. The funny thing was, I knew the person hadn't just called someone else, because anyone they could've contacted was sitting around that table with me. Then, I got *another* phone call from someone looking for a prom limousine. This time, instead of saying I was booked and giving the caller Darwin's number, I asked the caller if Darwin could call him. Happily, the person said, "That would be great," and gave me his phone number. Darwin booked the prom run.

I was once in a seminar where the speaker suggested that, when closing a sale, you give the prospect two to five business cards and ask them to give them to people they know. I thought about the prom caller and how, even though I gave Darwin's number, they still didn't call him. But if they gave their permission and phone number first, the sale was made.

The fallback to just giving someone your business card is that person must always have it on them to give it to someone else...and then there's the probability of the card getting lost and completely forgotten.

When you give someone your business card, make one small change. Don't just give someone the card and ask them to have someone call you; give someone your business card and ask them to get the person's *permission* for you to call them. You will have control over making the first point of contact, and you'll radically increase your number of closed sales.

"Pretend that every single person you meet has a sign around his or her neck that says, 'Make me feel important.' Not only will you succeed in sales, you will succeed in life."

– Mary Kay Ash

The true power of a system is what it will produce without you running it.

CHAPTER 11:
DEVELOPING BRAND RECOGNITION

Defining Your Brand

According to Webster's dictionary, a brand or brand name is a "word, name, or symbol, etc., especially one legally registered as a trademark, used by a manufacturer or merchant to identify its products distinctively from others of the same type and usually prominently displayed on its goods, in advertising, etc."

The strength of a business can often depend upon the effectiveness of its brand name. There are certain key points that should be considered when choosing your logo, brand, or brand name. How memorable is it? Can you recall it after only seeing it a few times? Is it easily confused with other brands or logos? Is it easy to see and recognize from a distance? (When my kids were little, they could spot a Toys"R"Us from three blocks away.) Is it easily transferrable to different types of marketing, like a card, trifold, postcard, or website? Do the colors have the feeling you want your business to have? Is your brand just words, a picture, or both? (There's one store that does a picture logo very well: Target.)

Now let's take a look at your brand's message. If you currently have a brand, does it fully describe your mission? When thinking about your mission in regard to competition, remember that competition is only as strong as we allow it to be. Case in point: Apple. One could argue that Apple has a lot of competition, yet not really. Apple has branded itself by creating a culture behind their products. People will stand in line for hours to buy the latest iPhone or MacBook, not just because they want the product, but because they want to be part of the Apple community. Steve Jobs focused on the *why* (not just the *what*) behind the product. That's why the iPod beat its competition: Jobs focused on why people would want the device, not just what it did. We all know the infamous iPod tagline: "A thousand songs in your pocket."

Another great example is Band-Aid. Because they repeatedly reached us via ongoing advertising, years later, if you cut yourself, you'll think to yourself, *Ouch, I need a Band-Aid.* Even though there are many similar products on the market, the entire market itself is named after their brand name. And of course, it's a given that golden arches mean McDonald's is nearby. Close your eyes and see if you can recall ten logos or brand names off the top of your head. My guess is you can.

Your brand needs to be personal. Why do you do what you do? This takes us back to your purpose, dream, or "why." What is one word, thought, or picture that best describes that? Your brand also needs to have market stickability. When people see your brand, they have to be able to recognize it right away—and that should inspire excitability in them.

Often people will become emotionally attached to a brand or logo of a company they frequently do business with. This will sometimes make a mom-and-pop-business's expansion or "selling out" such a painful experience. But sometimes these smaller businesses will simply sell their logo, rename themselves, and continue on as usual—and this can greatly financially benefit that business and its customers. This is an example of the true power of brands: a small company can sell a name or logo for half a million dollars, and their little lovable business will never miss a beat or alter their standards of service.

When I was building Newcastle Limousine, I looked at what made us stand out among all the other limousine companies. "Newcastle" helped because it was the name of an old mining town that many locals considered a part of their history. But what else? Was it our cars? Was it our chauffeurs? Their uniform, training, the way they made our clients feel? How did I want our clients to remember us? How did I stand apart, positively, from my competition? In other words, why would someone rent from my company instead of the other ones?

I sat down and listed my company's strong points next to my competitors'. Below are those lists.

Newcastle Limousine	The Competition
Newer fleet	Older fleet
Different sized limousines	Smaller fleet
4,6,8,and 10 passengers	only 4,6,or 10 passengers
Professionally trained chauffeurs	Anyone they can find to drive for them
Well-dressed chauffeurs in black uniforms	No standardized uniform
Midrange in price	Higher priced
Limousines kept very clean	Limousines would show up dirty
Ice and water in limousines	No ice and water in the limousine
Chauffeurs have a manual that they follow	Chauffeurs did things their way

Once I figured out my company's strengths, I needed to find a way to build my brand around them. I knew I needed to earn a piece of my clients' hearts. It was important that my clients had a personal interest in the success of my company. Otherwise, why would they refer me to others? I also knew that I needed to stay in front of my clients on a consistent basis so they would refer me. I started to implement different systems into my business designed around how we served our clients.

The logo was simple—the outline of a castle, with the tagline, "We are there when you need us." But what about stickability? Again, I had to keep my company and its logo in the forefront of their minds. I focused on creating an unforgettable experience. As I discussed in the previous chapter, I knew that if I could create brand loyalty around becoming a trusted advisor to my clients, provide professional chauffeurs, maintain a clean fleet, and provide my client-appreciation program on a monthly basis, my company would stand out among others. And it did. We averaged around five referrals a week.

Branding is not just about setting your products or services apart from others—it's more about obtaining emotional buy-in from your clients or customers by offering exceptional service and making them feel like they are royalty.

Newcastle Limousine had many regular customers. When booking their runs, I would always end the call by saying, "Great, John," or, "Great, Mary, I will see you Monday at seven." When I sold the company and we moved back to Wisconsin, I still answered the phones and booked the runs. For six months I still ended calls that way. Yet, over the six months, even though someone else would pick them up, no one ever said, "Hey, Mike, where were you?" Most knew that I was in Wisconsin, but when I said, "See you Monday at seven," no one ever questioned it.

That showed me that even though I heard myself saying, "Great, Mary. See you Monday at seven," Mary heard, "On Monday at seven, there will be a clean town car with a well-dressed chauffeur there to pick you up." That's the power of a well-run system.

CHAPTER 12:
TIME MANAGEMENT

It amazes me how many people say, "If I only had more time," or, "There is never enough time in the day." Yet, whether a person is very successful, busy, or floundering, we all have the same twenty-four hours in a day. It's not a question of how much time there is, but how the time is spent. One of the biggest killers of time management is lack of focus.

A while back I was sitting in a seminar, and the speaker took out a large jar and filled it with rocks. He then asked the audience if the jar was full. Most of the people in the audience said yes. The speaker then pulled out a bucket of pebbles and poured them over the rocks. Shaking the jar, he asked the audience if the jar was full now.

Now not as many people in the audience said yes. The speaker pulled out a bucket full of sand and continued to pour it over the rocks and pebbles, again shook the jar, asking the audience if the jar was full. By now the audience was starting to catch on and nobody said yes. The speaker then pulled out a jar full of water and poured it over the sand, pebbles, and rocks. The speaker then asked the audience, "If I'd poured the water or pebbles in first, would the rocks fit?"

You see, with time management, it works the same way. Most people begin their day by pouring the sand, water, or pebbles into their schedule and don't leave room for the rocks (the most important tasks of your day). The pebbles, sand, and water represent everything less-important in your day.

When planning for your day or week, do your "rock" things first, then move on to the next most-important things (pebbles), and the next, and the next, until you're done. Steven Covey's book *The Seven Habits of Highly Effective People* talks about four quadrants he lists as, "high urgency high importance, high urgency low importance, low urgency high importance, low urgency low importance."

To illustrate these different quadrants, let's say you're having a dinner party, and you have four hours to get ready. You don't have anything for dessert. The meat you're cooking for the party is still frozen. You have a friend who needs your help with a report that is due next Friday. Your car needs its oil changed. Your mom needs your help moving a box from the sunroom to the garage. You need to get your hair cut. You have a customer who is waiting for a part that you said you would drop off by the end of the week. You need to get cash to pay the people coming to help you with the party. And you still have a report that needs to go out before the end of the day, sitting on your desk waiting to be signed. What do you do? You can't get it all done by the end of the day—or can you? Let's review the list below.

> High urgency High importance
> High urgency Low importance
> Low urgency High importance
> Low urgency Low importance

How would you tackle the things you need to do? Let's first start by creating a list of all that needs to be done. Remember your big rocks, or the main things that need your focus at the moment. You're having a dinner party and you have four hours to get ready. How do they rank?

- ✓ You don't have anything for dessert—High urgency High importance
- ✓ The meat you're cooking for the party is still frozen—High urgency High importance
- ✓ You have a friend who needs your help with a report that is due next Friday—Low urgency Low importance
- ✓ Your car needs its oil changed—Low urgency High importance
- ✓ You need to get your hair cut—Low urgency Low importance

✓ You have a customer who is waiting for a part that you said you would drop off by the end of the week—Low urgency High importance

✓ Your mom needs your help moving a box from the sunroom to the garage—Low urgency High importance

✓ You need to get cash to pay the people coming to help you with the party—High urgency High importance

✓ You still have a report that needs to go out before the end of the day, sitting on your desk waiting to be signed—High urgency High importance

Now that they are listed by level of importance, put them in a list by priority. It's one in the afternoon on a Wednesday, and the party is starting at five.

o You still have a report that needs to go out before the end of the day, sitting on your desk waiting to be signed. *It only takes a minute to sign and then it will be out of the way. If you wait until later, you might forget to sign it.*

o The meat you're cooking for the party is still frozen. *This will take the most time to complete.*

o You need to get cash to pay the people coming to help you with the party. *This involves leaving and going to the bank, and because it's your account, you can't have someone else do it for you. And since you'll be out, you can pick up dessert on your way home.*

o You don't have anything for dessert. *You picked it up on your way back from the bank. The rest you could put off until the next day.*

o You have a customer who is waiting for a part that you said you would drop off by the end of the week.

o *If your costumer is on the way, you could swing by his office after getting dessert. Otherwise, drop it off the next day.*

o Your mom needs your help moving a box from the sunroom to the garage. *You could help your mom after the party.*

- o Your car needs its oil changed. *You can fit this in around other things you need to do. Many places will change your oil while you wait.*
- o You need to get your hair cut. *This you can also do while you're out and about as time allows. Again, because it's not urgent, you could put it off until the next day or so.*
- o You have a friend who needs your help with a report that is due next Friday. *You have plenty of time to do this later in the week.*

How people react to these different quadrants will help them determine their level of efficiency with time management. Many people simply react to their days' events. They go from event to event, fire to fire, without stopping to assess the importance of what they're doing. People will spend a majority of their time working on activities that aren't the most important. Goal setting is so imperative because having clear business goals will help determine which activities are the most important.

Make a list of all the things that you either want to do or need to do in order to move your business goals or objectives to the next level. Then pick the top three activities necessary to move those goals to the next level. Write them down on a sheet of paper. Now focus one-hundred percent on those activities or goals until they are finished. Then pick the next most-important activities or goals and complete them. Then move on to the next three, and so on, until the goal or objective is completed.

Another great tool for planning your time is to set out your week the week before it. Review your day the day before. I once shared with a mentor that I wanted to book a minimum of five new appointments and five follow-ups a week. He told me to make sure I had my appointments scheduled and written in my calendar by Friday for the upcoming week, then I could enjoy the weekend. Otherwise, I would have to make as many calls on Saturday as needed to ensure that I met my goal. When I accomplished this goal, my next week went very smoothly.

Another huge time-killer is trying to do everything yourself. One of the hardest (yet most important) things to master in business is learning to delegate things out to others. In business, there are only two reasons for you to do something yourself: only you can do it, or you can't afford to have someone else do it.

A mentor once told me to discover what it is I enjoy doing and do well (the two often go hand-in-hand...I find most people enjoy doing what they're good at). He then advised me to surround myself with people whose strengths were my weaknesses. There are only so many hours in a day, but when we delegate tasks to other people, we are in a way borrowing their hours, which allows us to get a lot more done.

Here is a list of questions to ask yourself concerning time management.

Questions on Time Management

1. How do I prioritize my tasks?

2. How do I process my tasks?

3. Do I check tasks off my list once they are completed?

4. Who is responsible for scheduling my time?

5. Do I review my tasks on a daily basis?

6. How are new tasks added to my schedule?

7. How do I monitor activities on a daily basis?

8. How are appointments processed?

9. Who's responsible for setting my appointments?

10. How are my appointments confirmed, and who confirms them?

11. Do I have a daily schedule? And how well do I follow it?

12. How do I monitor my daily production?

13. How do I organize my day so I can accomplish my responsibilities?

14. How do I keep on-track in terms of my core tasks?

The answers to these questions will help lay the ground rules for how you manage your time. Just remember: time is your most valuable asset, so don't waste it!

"Congruency between your vision and your action will determine whether you are a visionary or a dreamer."

— Steve Siebold

"The future belongs to those who believe in the beauty of their dreams."

— Eleanor Roosevelt

CHAPTER 13:
TURNING DREAMS INTO REALITY

Consistent goal-setting is the cornerstone to achieving all great dreams in both business and life. Children are always dreaming of something big, yet, as adults, we often set limitations on ourselves. Consistently setting goals will set the pathway to many great accomplishments.

Children do this instinctually when they come to us and say, "Mom, Dad, when I grow up, I want to be a fireman." Or they might say they want to be an astronaut, a teacher, or even a superhero. Usually, they come up with meaningful occupations. Unfortunately, as they grow, they tend to shy away from such dreams.

I always cringe when I hear a parent say, "Oh, Tommy, stop playing make-believe. It's time for you to grow up," or, "You know that you will never be able to do that." Phrases like that are the destroyers of all great intentions and imagination. Make-believe is the place where all great accomplishments are born. As parents, it's essential that we encourage our children to shoot for the stars, set goals, and chase after their dreams. And it is equally important that we do it ourselves, too.

It's important to establish a deadline or benchmark, even if it's way off in the future. A goal is far more effective when it is written down, for what gets written down gets done.

A goal also needs to be *measurable.* We all need to be able to measure our progress. Especially if it's a large goal set way off in the future. It helps to take a large goal and break it up into smaller mini-goals.

I remember my daughter coming home from a doctor's appointment when she was about two. She said to my wife and me, "Mommy, Daddy, when I grow up, I'm going to be a doctor."

We both looked at her and said, "That's great, Sabrina. You'll make a wonderful doctor." Later that week, I bought Sabrina a small doctor's kit from Toys"R"Us as a reminder of her new goal. All of her stuffed animals got physicals the next day. Before long, there wasn't a sick stuffed animal anywhere to be found. Years passed, yet her dream to become a doctor still remained, even though it took on different forms.

When Sabrina was about eight, she looked at Jennifer and said, "Mommy, I decided that I am going to open a clinic near your office. That way, if you get sick, you can come to my clinic during your lunch hour."

Smiling, Jennifer said, "That's wonderful, Sabrina. That will be so convenient. And I'll get a discount, too, because I'm your mother, right?"

"I guess I could give you a ten percent discount." Sabrina said, looking somewhat annoyed.

"What? Only ten percent? But I'm your mother."

"Yeah, Mom, but I have to pay everyone who works there, the person who checks you in, and the nurse who takes your blood pressure. That's a lot of people."

"Hey, a ten percent discount is better than what we are getting now, Jennifer. Besides, you'll be able to go there on your lunch hour." I said, laughing.

We knew then that her dream of becoming a doctor was still burning strong. About a year later, Sabrina and I were at a networking event, and I overheard her asking Monty, one of my clients who was a residential homebuilder, if he would consider helping her build a building when she grew up, near where her mother worked.

Surprised, Monty asked her, "What is the building for?"

"Oh, I want to open a clinic near my mom's office, and when I heard you and my dad talking about the house you just built, I was thinking that if I can't find a building that fits my needs, then I could just build one." Sabrina replied.

"Well, Sabrina, I normally only build houses, but for you, I'll make an exception," Monty said, looking at me and smiling.

"Thanks, Monty. I look forward to doing business with you in the future," Sabrina replied, a big smile plastered on her face.

I'm not sure what surprised me more: that fact that we were having this conversation, or that it seemed so natural.

That's what's so great about how kids think. They don't get caught up in all the details; they see a picture of what they want, and the rest is expected to come naturally.

As far as Sabrina was concerned, the deal was as good as done and didn't need any further thought until she was ready to open the clinic.

I, on the other hand, was thinking to myself, *Sabrina needs to finish medical school, which she needs to pay for first. Then she needs to create a business plan for her clinic and make sure there is a viable market for it. After all, Jennifer doesn't get sick very often...then, after searching for a suitable location to lease, if there isn't anything available, she would have to acquire a suitable lot, do all the engineering work, and finally, one- to two-million dollars later, she would be ready to build a building...*

Boy, I was already tired just thinking about it! And what were the chances of Sabrina still wanting to be a doctor when she grew up?

Another great thing about kids is that they don't let fear or doubt get in the way. They set a goal and go for it. Whether old or young, if we have a dream or a goal and can see its final state, we can bring our dreams into reality. It may take time, a lot of work, or even the help of many other people...but if the desire is strong enough, it can be done.

I often tell our kids they can't always control the results, but they *can* control their actions. The right actions will, in time, yield the results they want.

Sabrina played the flute for the Milwaukee Youth Symphony Orchestra and set a goal to join the Philharmonic Orchestra, which was very hard to get into. She had to try out and then wait about a month before she knew if she got in. The day the results arrived, Sabrina was having lunch with a friend who was already in the Philharmonic Orchestra.

Two letters came to the house, and knowing how important it was to my daughter, I took them straight to her.

Sabrina opened the first letter and saw that she had gotten into a group called Chamber Flutes. Sabrina then opened the second letter and sat there with tears running down her cheeks.

"Why, Dad, why? I wanted to get into the Philharmonic Orchestra so badly."

"I know, Sabrina."

"I got wait-listed. Why? I practiced so much!"

"I don't know, Sabrina. What I do know is that in life we get three answers: yes, no, or not now. It's not 'yes' because you didn't get in yet. It's not 'no' because you're wait-listed. So that just means that it's *not now*. Maybe you will have to wait until next year or maybe later this year. Remember, you can't always control the results, but you can control your actions."

After a moment, I said, "Do me a favor, Sabrina." I hugged her and continued, "You have Chamber Flutes from four-thirty to six on Mondays, and the Philharmonic Orchestra practices from six-thirty to nine on Mondays. Right?"

"Yes, Dad, that's right."

"Since you're going to be there anyway, go to the Philharmonic Orchestra, help set up, talk with your friends, and envision how you would feel and what you would do if you were in the orchestra, okay?"

"Okay, Dad."

The first week of practice came, and Sabrina helped set up. Her friends came in and she talked and joked around with them. She stood where she would've stood if she had gotten into the orchestra. She visualized how she would feel if she were part of it. When it was time for practice to start, we had to leave.

Sabrina walked out, looking at the ground sadly. The second week came and we repeated the process, and again, when it was time for the orchestra to start, Sabrina solemnly left. The third week came, and again, when the orchestra started, Sabrina left looking crushed.

I was starting to second-guess myself. I couldn't help thinking that I might be unintentionally setting Sabrina up for continued disappointment. I hated seeing her so down in the dumps. I asked Sabrina if she liked setting up and hanging out with her friends.

She answered, "Yes, but I really wish I could stay and play with the orchestra."

I told her to be patient and her turn would come.

The following week, Sabrina was at a swim meet. While I was waiting for her, I got a call from the senior conductor of the Philharmonic Orchestra: "Mike, I opened up another seat for Sabrina, and I would really like for her to play with us." Then he asked if she would still like to be part of the orchestra.

I said, "Yes, she has been praying every day for this opportunity. I will let her know and we will see you on Monday."

"Great, I look forward to seeing Sabrina next week," he said.

Not only did she finish out the year in the Philharmonic Orchestra, she even won a contest and composed a piece for the Chamber Flutes.

In 2012, she got into the highest level of the Milwaukee Youth Symphony Orchestra called Senior Symphony. This past summer, they toured Vienna and Prague and represented the United States in an international music contest, where they placed second in the world.

We can't always control our results. However, we can control our activities. When we do the right activities (although it may take time, patience, and the help of other people), in time we will receive our desired results.

Once visualized, goals are very powerful motivators. The only challenge that both adults and children face when they have a really large goal is that it can become overwhelming. It's hard to determine what to do first. The first step to avoid being overwhelmed is to visualize the goal in its completed stage. The next step is to back-engineer the steps to the beginning.

My youngest daughter, Monica, has wanted a puppy for about two years. About once a month, she would ask us for a puppy.

Jennifer always answered, "No, Monica, we already have three fish. A puppy is too much work."

A few months ago, Monica found a really cute puppy and brought a picture to show us. "Mom, Dad, look at this puppy. It's so cute, and it only costs $750. Can I get it? Please, please, can I get it? I'll pay for it."

Now, when your fourteen-year-old daughter says "only $750" when referring to a dog (puppy or not), that should be the first reason to worry.

Jennifer looked at Monica and said, "$750, huh? And you will pay for it?"

"Yes, only $750. I'll pay for it and we can pick it up in four weeks."

"Okay, tell you what," Jennifer replied, "You have three weeks to come up with the money, and you can't take any out of your bank account. You have to raise the money from scratch."

"Really? Then I can have my puppy?"

"That's correct," Jennifer said.

"Okay, Mom, let me fill this out and then please sign it."

Monica, understanding the power of a well-orchestrated contract, grabbed a pen and wrote out: *I, Jennifer Raber, will let Monica Raber buy her puppy if she can raise the money within three weeks.*

Jennifer signed the sheet and gave it back to Monica. I think that Jennifer secretly hoped Monica would say, "Raise $750 in three weeks? That's impossible. Okay, I guess I can't have the puppy."

Jennifer must've forgotten that we'd always instilled very entrepreneurial values in our children.

Monica started back-engineering her goal: $750 in three weeks. That would be $250 a week, or $35.71 a day. If she could sell one Moonjar® for a profit of $5, she would have to sell a total of 150 Moonjars®, or 50 Moonjars® a week—or 7.14 Moonjars® a day.

Later that day, Monica called the breeder and negotiated him down to $650. She then asked me if she could go to different networking meetings with me so she could sell the Moonjars®. I agreed, and she was able to raise the money in just short of three weeks. Monica is now the proud owner of a black Cockapoo puppy, who just so happens to be sleeping on the floor next to me as I write this. Thank you, Monica, for persevering and bringing your goal into reality...because Lucy really is the cutest puppy.

Always remember: the true growth lies in the journey, not just reaching the goal.

Goal-Setting as a Group

Another great tool for helping us reach our goals, especially if they involve other people, is to set a group or family goal.

When Sabrina was nine and Monica and Sam were six, we wanted to attend a three-day conference called Mastermind, an annual event put on by Brian Buffini. One year, it was scheduled to take place at Disney World in Florida. As a family, we decided our goal was to attend the event. This meant we would need to save the money to pay for the trip well before going to Florida. We figured it would cost around $3,000 for the family...that was the amount we set as our savings goal.

Every Sunday, we would review our budget and see how much we had put toward our goal.

One day, I got home and asked my family, "How does takeout pizza sound for tonight?"

Sabrina looked up and said, "Yeah, pizza sounds great, but is pizza in the budget?"

Stunned, I answered, "No, pizza isn't in the budget, but I'm tired and don't feel like making dinner tonight. Pizza sounds good, right?"

"Mastermind, Dad. Remember Mastermind? We'll all help you make dinner tonight," all three kids chimed in.

I hadn't even considered Mastermind, but for the kids, the desire to go to Florida and Disney World was much more powerful than pizza.

Several months later, all five of us went to Disney World and the Mastermind event. The trip was paid for before we got on the plane, and Sabrina, Monica, and Sam each had $50 to spend when we got there. Never once did they ask if Jennifer or I could pay for something they wanted. They were very careful not to buy souvenirs until the last day so that they could spend their $50 wisely on what they truly wanted.

There is no greater feeling as a parent or leader for than knowing that you've given your children or companions the self-reliance to make wise financial decisions—whether that decision involves purchasing a 50-cent piece of candy, a souvenir from a gift shop, or a new car. It's important to teach everyone the difference between needs and wants early on. The earlier they learn to manage their money, the easier it will be for them to acquire wealth, which begins with setting goals and reverse-engineering the necessary steps to achieve those goals.

The Power of The Written Goal

When establishing goals, nothing is more powerful than putting them into writing. I believe the reason that New Year's

Resolutions fail is that they're not written down. In my experience, once things are put into writing, they tend to be accomplished. To really add momentum to your goal, include a picture or photo next to the words to help you visualize your goal more powerfully.

Here are just a few of the reasons to put your goals into writing. Written goals

- Create a sense of purpose and anticipation
- Are great confidence builders
- Help strengthen focus and reduce time-wasting
- Reduce subconscious conflicts or objections
- Provide guidelines for good decisions
- Help you work through mistakes and obstacles you might encounter
- Strengthen your resolve to accomplish the goals

Putting your goals on paper helps to bring out your abilities and competencies to accomplish them.

When setting your goals, it's important to have a deadline set. Also imagine or visualize what it will feel like to accomplish that goal. Be aware of *why* you want to accomplish that goal, for that will help you overcome self-imposed or outside objections.

There are different ways to write your goals down. One way is to make a list, and another is to write your goals out in present tense, as if you have already achieved them. For example: "It is January 31st, I am 190 pounds, full of energy, and in excellent shape."

You can also use a great tool referred to as a dream board. You cut out pictures of things you want or want to become. Here is an example of one.

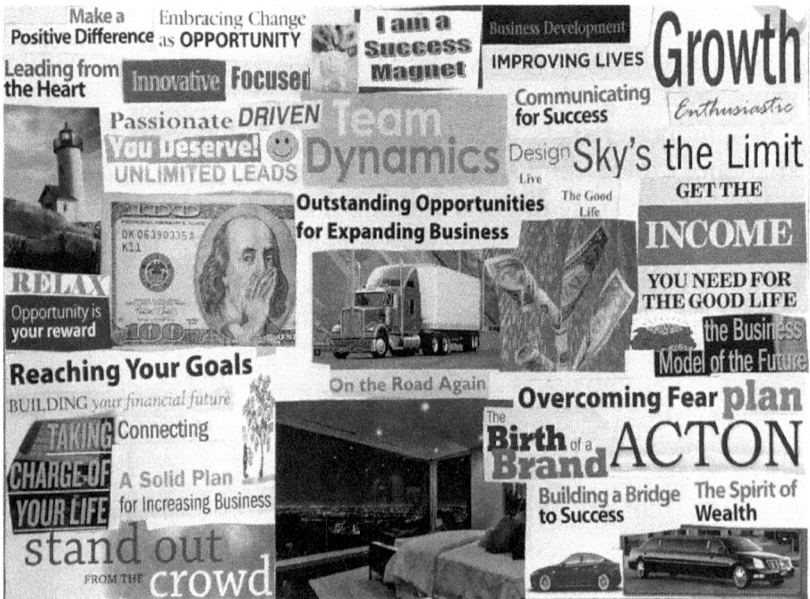

To help assist you in the completion of your business goals, I have included a list of questions around goal-setting. Please take the time to go through the list and answer the different questions. You'll be well on your way to moving your business to the next level and seeing great things happen in your business.

Questions on Goal Setting

1. When I reach my business and personal goals, what will they look like in one, three, and five years?

2. How will my business look, feel, and act in five years?

3. What changes am I willing to make in order to fulfill my life's work?

4. How do I define the next level of my business?

5. Am I financially prepared to obtain my goals?

6. Am I willing to do what it takes to obtain my goals?

7. Am I willing to learn the disciplines necessary in order to move my business to the next level?

8. What will that look like?

9. What price am I willing pay in order to obtain my business goals?

10. How long will I keep working in order to obtain them?

11. What obstacles, pitfalls, and traps will I encounter along the way?

12. How many hours a day should I spend studying, working, etc., in order to reach my business goals?

13. What is my most effective method of studying?

14. What types of training should I be focusing on?

15. What's the costliest mistake I have to avoid in terms of obtaining my business goals?

16. How will I monitor my own activities?

17. Is there someone who will hold me accountable to the steps necessary to reach my business goals?

18. How often do I review my goals?

19. How much time do I spend reviewing and projecting my business goals on a daily basis?

20. Are they memorized?

21. Are they written down?

22. How many business goals do I currently have?

23. How many of my business goals are short-term and long-term goals?

24. How many and what kind of business goals should I concentrate on?

25. What is my "why" or purpose behind my business, and how do my goals fit into that purpose?

26. Can I outline in detail the system I have for organizing, reviewing, and completing my goals?

27. How many new business goals do I set each month on average?

28. How many goals should I set based on my long-term objectives?

29. Can I lay out a plan showing how I'm going to reach my business goals?

30. When talking to other people, how do I present a plan for achieving my business goals?

31. How much time do I spend planning and working on goal-setting?

32. What kinds of resources do I hire to assist in reaching my business goals?

33. What kind of return do I receive from obtaining my business goals?

34. Have I created any relationships with people who have similar goals?

35. Once a new business goal is set, how is it processed? Do I have a goal completion check list?

36. How often do I sit down and go over my business goals?

37. What percent of my time is spent working on my business goals or business plan during a normal work week?

My goal for these questions is to give you thinking-points for not only helping you with setting your goals, but also with your business plan. A good business plan should address a lot of the questions mentioned in this chapter.

SECTION THREE

THE SYSTEM

SIMPLE STEPS TO CREATING A SOLID BUSINESS AND FINANCIAL FOUNDATION

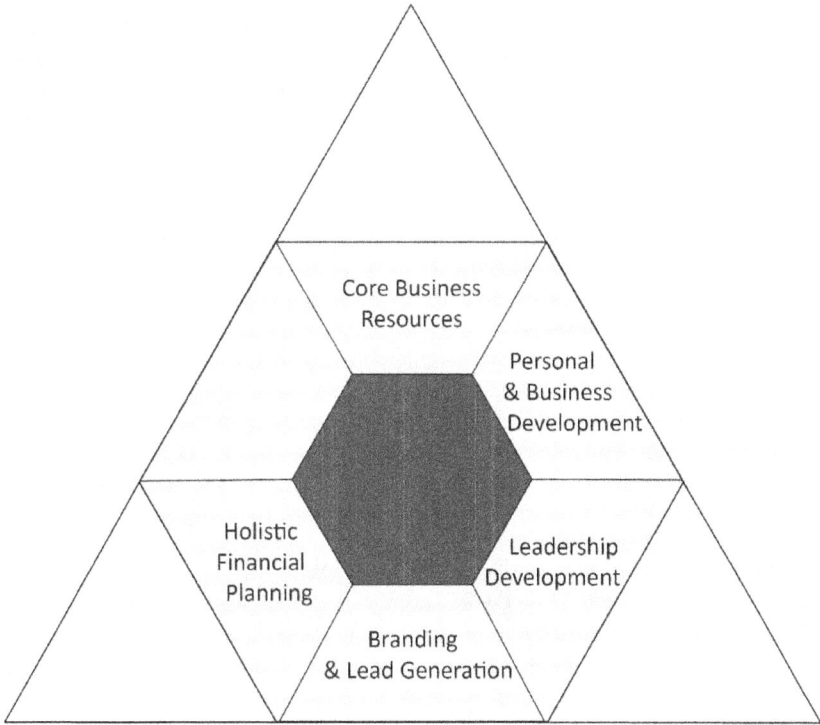

Core Business
Resources

Personal
& Business
Development

Holistic
Financial
Planning

Leadership
Development

Branding
& Lead Generation

CHAPTER 14:
TAKING THE CHAOS OUT OF
FINANCIAL MANAGEMENT

Creating a Living Budget

When you set out to build a successful business, you will need to have a strong financial foundation. The first and most important part of that foundation is implementing a solid and consistent money-management system. The two most important tools used for maintaining a money management system are a **living budget** and a **net worth statement**. Once you have a living budget and a net worth statement in place, it's important to start looking at your goals and how much money you need to reach those goals.

I've found that when most people hear the words "financial planning" or "money management," they associate them with accounting or bookkeeping. They might also find themselves saying something like, "Sure, financial planning is important if you have a lot of money, but I don't have very much money, so what's the difference?" Or, "I don't need to worry about a budget or a financial plan yet. I don't have that many expenses, and I always have enough money to cover my expenses." Or, "Sure, money management is important, but I don't have the time now to worry about it."

On the surface, these statements might sound reasonable. However, your success depends upon the degree of your planning. You've probably heard the saying, "If you fail to plan, you are planning to fail," or, according to Jim Rohn, "The difference between the rich and the poor is that the rich invest their money and spend what's left, while the poor spend their money and invest what's left." True financial and business planning is not just action—it is a mindset, as well.

All living creatures understand that survival requires putting food away for harder times. Squirrels spend all summer collecting nuts and burying them for winter. Bears hibernate in the winter so that they don't burn too much body fat while food is scarce. But, as consumers, many human beings live for today and forget to plan for tomorrow.

I often tell clients that if they continue to manage their money and businesses the same way they did last year, their finances and business will look the same next year. If that is okay with them, that's great. However, if they want more, they need to change what they are doing today. In other words, are they on or off track to reach their business or financial goals and making their dreams come true?

Many people don't like budgets because they consider them limiting. However, a budget is a scoreboard that shows you how your financial outflow compares to your inflow at any given point in time. Most people wouldn't drive in a foreign city without getting a map or directions, so why would they run their most valuable resources without a financial roadmap?

Years back, Brian Buffini, the founder of Buffini and Company, suggested that I refer to a budget as a **living budget**, which is a term I really like—it's important to create a budget that flexes around your lifestyle. Your budget or spending plan is the vehicle that gets you from point A to point B financially, and money is the gas that fuels the vehicle. How much you make isn't as important as how much you save and spend. It's very important to always watch for spillage in your spending. When you don't know how much or little you really have, there is no way of knowing how much you can actually afford to spend.

Your budget acts as a general guideline, but it's important that you assess where your spending is within your budget at least once a month. Make necessary adjustments after that. As an example, let's say you spend on average $400 a month on food. That is where you set your budget. You then have guests from out of town who stay with you for two weeks. You may end up spending $500 that month on food. So, that month, you need to make an adjustment for food in your budget. Otherwise, it might feel like you just blew your budget, when really you just needed to account for an increase in food costs.

I have found that many people don't set reasonable expectations when creating their budgets, so they continue blowing it month after month and eventually give up. When you implement a financial management system, it needs to give you a greater sense of control, otherwise it becomes restrictive and frustrating—not freeing.

When you begin the process of creating your financial management system, the first tool you need to put in place is that living budget. Your budget should be made up of two parts: **incoming money or income**, and **outgoing money or expenses**.

As an entrepreneur, whether you own a business or are self-employed (and your pay is commission-based by your sales or production), your income will often be inconsistent by nature. Establishing a sense of consistency can be an even bigger challenge in these cases, because you may not always know how much you will be getting or when it will be coming in. Therefore, it is not only extremely important that you have a budget for your business, it's also critical that you have a personal budget. I would suggest that you pay yourself a salary that covers your living expenses, charity, and other investments. It's very important, however, that this money management system be treated as a business expense. As a business owner, your goal is to get to the point where your salary and business expenses are lower than your net business income.

For example, let's say your business brings in a monthly gross income of $10,000. Your monthly business operating expenses are $4,000. Therefore, your business's net monthly income is $6,000. If your monthly personal living expenses are $5,000, then pay yourself a salary of $5,000. This leaves a surplus in your business of $1,000.00

Once your net business profit is consistently showing a positive return, your business is at the point where it will start helping you build your wealth. It can also start to get tricky, though, because you want to pay yourself enough to cover your living expenses, have enough extra for charity, and to invest in your retirement plan. You still need to make sure you keep enough working capital in the business to maintain a strong cash flow for your business. When you're starting or growing your business, liquidity is especially important to the lifeblood of the business.

It's important to discuss the process of separating your business income from your personal income at this point. Once that is done, you need to create a living budget for both your personal and business expenses. One of the biggest mistakes new entrepreneurs make is not having a personal budget, so their personal expenses slowly eat away at their business.

The type of system you use will depend a lot on the size and type of business you have. For illustrative purposes, I'm going to use a small startup company in which the owner may be self-employed—someone who works for him- or herself, but is part of a larger company. Examples would be realtors, doctors, those who are traditionally independent contractors, or someone who owns a small traditional business.

The system that works best is setting up a separate account, either a business or a personal account that you treat like a business account. It's always better to have a *regular* business account, but if you have only a few sales or lower revenue coming into your business at first, it may not make sense to start with a business account due to higher cost. In that case, open another personal account, but treat it as if it were a business account.

Often your bank will allow you to assign nicknames to your different accounts, so you could give it your business's name to help you differentiate it from the other accounts. The most important part: only business revenue should go into this account and business expenses should come out of it.

As your business revenue or income flows in, you'll want to deposit it into your business account. You'll then take an amount you can consistently pay out and pay yourself once or twice a month, as if it were part of your salary.

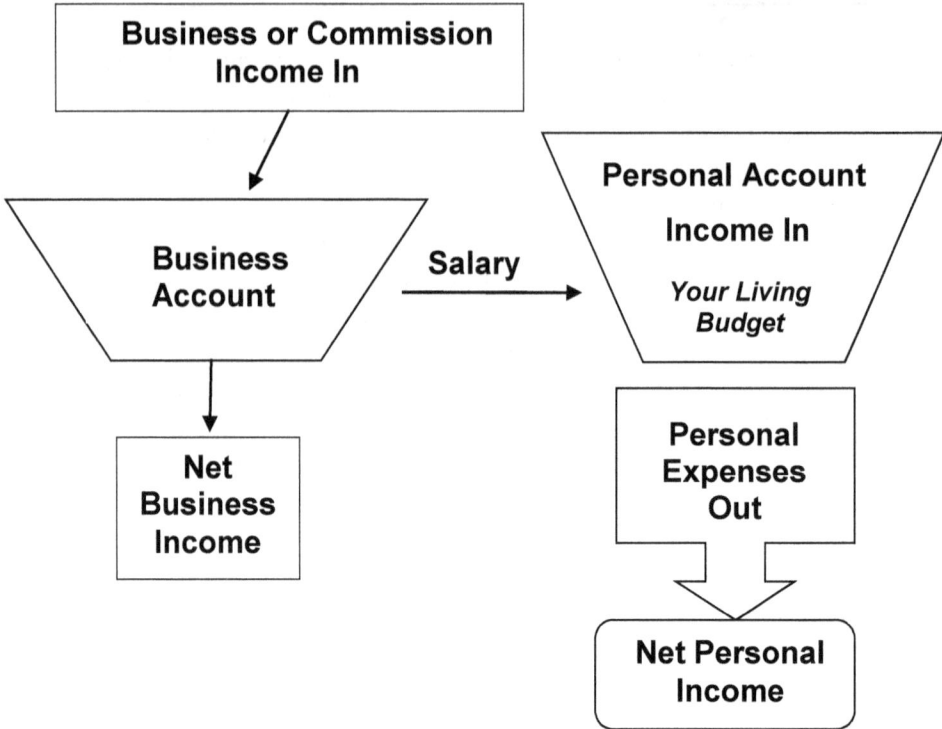

As you complete the budget for your business, you will need to track your business expenses. You may also want to put a percentage aside for charity, and it's a good idea to apply a percentage towards a business saving/investing account. In essence, you will follow the same system for your business as you would for your personal financial management system.

Treat your business as if it were an independent person, completely separate from yourself. The purpose of the business is to support you. Go to www.entrepreneurshipthatmakescents.com and download the spreadsheets for preparing your business and personal budget.

For your business, I recommend that you use the following formula: a good rule of thumb is to keep your operating expenses to around 30% of your gross revenue. If at all possible, set a goal to keep the remainder of your expenses, including your salary, between 40 and 50% of your gross revenue. For the sake of this illustration, we are going to assume that your total business expenses are 70% of your gross revenue, leaving a net profit of 30%. You would then take that 30% profit and apply it to your business's financial management system. It would look like this:

> Gross revenue: $1,000.00
> Operating expense: $300.00 or 30%
> Other expenses: $400.00 or 40%
> Net profit: $300.00 or 30%

I recommend that you take the 30% net profit and divide it up this way: 10% of your net income, or $30.00 ($300 x 10% equals $30.00) and apply it to charity. I have found that it is equally beneficial for businesses to give back to the community. Plus, charitable contributions are often tax deductible, which can positively affect your tax situation. When making contributions, I suggest getting the opinion of a tax professional.

Some businesspeople take 10% of their gross revenue and apply it toward charity. This can be very daunting to people, particularly new business owners. It will likely be easier to commit to 10% of your net business revenue. As a business owner, this is a personal decision, so go with what best fits your beliefs and your business plan.

Then apply 30% of your net business profit, or $90.00 ($300.00 x 30% equals $90.00) toward short-term savings, business debt reduction, or your business emergency fund. Just as with your personal finances, it's a good idea to have three to six months of business expenses set aside for emergencies in a savings account. Then put 20% of your net profit ($60.00) into long-term savings/investments, and 20% ($60.00) into an account set aside for taxes. Then reinvest 20% ($60.00) back into your business.

A living budget is built around a consistent inflow and outflow of revenue and expenses, so when you have irregular income, it's even more important that you have a system in place to track your income and expenses.

Over the years of helping clients create their living budgets, I have found that no two budgets look alike. A living budget serves as an account of your ongoing revenue and expenses. However, it is also the foundation upon which to build your business. Many great business plans are smothered by unnecessary expenses.

When initially creating your living budget, list all your expenses on the Monthly Expenses Worksheet (Worksheet 101), as shown in the next couple of pages. You can also download a spreadsheet from our website. Then rank these expenses by their degree of importance.

I really like the system called "ABC-ing Your Expenses." I like this system because it allowed me to better prioritize my expenses and helped me to plug the leaks in my spending. Many of the things that I thought were "must-haves" were really "would-like-to-haves"—things I didn't really need.

Back when I was running Newcastle Limousine, I built the fleet up to six limousines and one town car. If you remember, my business expenses were around $15,000 a month. I was only averaging $7,500 a month in revenue. I was so busy in the day-to-day operations of the business that I had never stopped to create a budget. I maxed out the line of credit...and then a check bounced, then another, and another...and unfortunately, those checks were the lease payments on one of our limousines.

That day was my wake-up call. I went to a friend of mine and asked her what to do. She referred me to an event called The Turning Point Retreat®. I attended the event, and it truly became a turning point in my life. After the retreat, I was able to talk to the presenter, Brian Buffini. He told me that I needed to prepare both a business and personal budget, and then cut out anything that wouldn't affect my business adversely from week-to-week.

After running the numbers, I only really needed two limousines and one town car, given the number of limousine runs I was doing. The remaining vehicles were costing more to keep in our fleet each month than they were bringing in. So, I sold four of the limousines and opened a corporate account with a rental car company. That way I could rent a town car, van, or SUV only when I needed one.

That single change alone cut $6,000 a month in expenses out of my budget. I then made the commitment to build my business entirely by referral and canceled all our Yellow Pages advertisements, which cost $5,000 a month. I was now once again operating in the black.

Time to get back to creating your own living budget, or "spending plan," for those of you who think the word "budget" is a four-letter word. On the next couple pages, I will walk you through the process of creating a living budget from start to finish. There are several blank rows in case you have an expense that isn't on the expense worksheet. Just add it in the expense column. I would suggest that you print the worksheets and fill them out as your go through this exercise.

For the sake of the following exercise, I am only going to use six months of expenses. Ideally, you will want to go back twelve months. I have already added up each expense and placed them in the proper monthly expense slot. As stated previously, the first step in creating a living budget is to make a list of the things you spend money on, such as your mortgage or rent, food, insurance, utilities, entertainment, etc. On the following pages, you will find examples of both a blank and filled-in expense log. You can also go to our website, www.centsiblesolutions.com, and print the forms.

BLANK MONTHLY INCOME AND EXPENSE LOG

	Jan	Feb	March	April	May	June	Total
Salary							
TOTAL INCOME							
EXPENSES							
Household sup.							
Toiletries							
Food							
Mortgage							
Electricty / Gas							
Water & Sewer							
Phone / Internet							
Clothes							
Education							
Other Insurance							
Health Insurance							
Home Maintenance							
Furniture							
Donation							
Gas							
Auto Rapair							
Pharmacy							
Medical / Dental							
Presents / toys							
Travel							
Entertainment							
Property Tax							
Fed / State Tax							
Short term savings							
Long term savings							
Intrest / Bank fee							
TOTAL EXP.							
NET INCOME							

SAMPLE PREFILLED MONTHLY INCOME AND EXPENSE LOG

	Jan	Feb	March	April	May	June	Total
Salary	7,500.00	7,500.00	7,500.00	7,500.00	7,500.00	7,500.00	45,000.00
TOTAL INCOME	7,500.00	7,500.00	7,500.00	7,500.00	7,500.00	7,500.00	45,000.00
EXPENSES							
Household sup.		16.59				16.33	32.92
Toiletries	103.87	298.12	87.22	39.44	92.92	45	666.57
Food	336.22	816.93	482.79	458.87	606.82	502.67	3204.3
Mortgage	1594.64	1594.64	1594.64	1594.64	1594.64	1594.64	9567.84
Electricty / Gas	298.01	181.34	166.97	106.84	101.35	109.07	963.58
Water & Sewer			141.77			141.77	283.54
Phone / Internet	74.87	75.34	79.35	70.34	76.57	79.87	456.34
Clothes	18.96	92.69	301.57	258.87	518.93		1191.02
Education	79.5		364.58	375.23	28.64	76.71	924.66
Other Insurance	70.5		579.84	70.5		579.84	1300.68
Health Insurance	512.79	512.79	512.79	512.79	512.79	512.79	3076.74
Home Maintenance	11.61	175		31.38	66.72		284.71
Furniture		2100					2100
Donation	225	225	225	225	225	225	1350
Gas	281.37	262.35	304.23	337.39	294.3	284.49	1764.13
Auto Rapair	782.2					749.22	1531.42
Pharmacy	43.58	23.22	28.45	34	29.54	36.4	195.19
Medical / Dental	128			21.51			149.51
Presents / toys	50	22.69	30		171.06	50	323.75
Travel	53.31					408.53	461.84
Entertainment	89.35	110	70.79	123.78	89.78	129.28	612.98
Property Tax	3072.21		1576.19			1576.19	6224.59
Fed / State Tax				1060.8			1060.8
Short term savings	262.5	262.5	262.5	262.5	262.5	262.5	1575
Long term savings	262.5	262.5	262.5	262.5	262.5	262.5	1575
Intrest / Bank fee		50		25			75
TOTAL EXP.	8350.99	7081.7	7071.18	5871.38	4934.06	7642.8	40952.11
NET INCOME	-850.99	418.30	428.82	1,628.62	2,565.94	-142.80	4,047.89

With this worksheet, I pre-filled the slots assuming you had a monthly revenue of $7,500. You're living on 90% of your income, sharing 3% of your income (charitable donations), applying 3.5% to short-term savings, and putting 3.5% in long-term savings or debt reduction. I will discuss those percentages in a later chapter. Because saving and sharing follow your income, those are treated as variable expenses rather than fixed expenses, like rent or mortgage payments. I know this process can seem daunting at first, but I hope these worksheets will provide you with good guidelines.

Now back to the process. Once you have listed all your expenses, go through your checkbook, credit card statements, and bank statements. Add up all your expenses for the month in each category and write them in the Monthly Expense Log. Once you have all of your expenses listed on your Monthly Expense Log, add up the different months and put the amount in the total column.

Depending on the type of mortgage you might have, your property tax and homeowner's insurance may be escrowed or added to your monthly mortgage payment. If that is the case, then you won't have to put money aside for your property tax and homeowner's insurance. If you have the choice of paying the property tax and insurance yourself, I would recommend that you do so. That way you will have more control over when and how they are paid.

When lenders escrow property taxes and insurance, they always hold a couple months of extra payments aside. Depending on the amount of your property tax, that could mean a few thousand dollars. Over the course of the year, the interest you would earn on that extra amount could add up. Plus, if you should change lenders, that is easier to do so if you're in control of your payments. If you do pay taxes and insurance yourself, however, set aside the monthly allocation of your property tax payment so that you have it when it's time to make the payment. When you fill out your worksheet, you will see that some months you may have a negative balance. In January, for example, the first half of the property tax payment is required, and then the rest is payable over the next four months. There is also a large auto repair bill. To stay on track, it's also important to have an emergency fund in place, along with budgeting for things like your property tax.

I would recommend that you use the monthly expense log going forward to track all your expenses for the month. Once you have your monthly expenses written in the Monthly Expense Log, you can begin formulating your budget. When you do this again, I recommend going back at least six months—ideally a full year—so you can get a more accurate running average.

Here's how to find out how much you're spending, using your electric bill as an example. Month one: your bill is $298.01; month two: $181.34; month three: $166.97; month four: $106.84; month five: $101.35; and in month six, it's $109.07.

Total up these six months: $298.01 + $181.34 + $166.97 + $106.84 + $101.35 + $109.07 = $963.58. You should have $963.58 in your TOTAL column.

Like you just did with your electric bills, follow the same process for all your other expenses.

The next step is to take each expense out of the Total expense column on the Monthly Expense Log and carry it over to the Expense Worksheet 101, which is shown on the next page (or on our website).

Once you have all your different expense totals carried over to the Expense Worksheet, go through your expenses and decide if they are fixed, variable, irregular, or other expenses. In the Type column, add an "F" for a fixed expense, a "V" for a variable expense, an "I" for an irregular expense, and an "O" for another expense. Here are some definitions for clarity.

- **Fixed Expense**: Fixed expenses are amounts you have to pay every month that stay the same. Examples: your mortgage or rent, car loan, health insurance, child care, your savings plan, etc.
- **Variable Expense**: Variable expenses have to be paid every month, but the amount changes month-to-month. Examples: utilities, food, gas, entertainment, etc.
- **Irregular Expense**: Irregular expenses have to be paid quarterly, twice a year, or even annually. Examples: different types of insurance or property taxes. Depending on your city, you may have to pay them monthly, every two months over the first six months of the year, or even twice a year.
- **Other Expense**: Other expenses tend to be a one-time payments, or expenses that are infrequent. Examples: a family trip you take once a year, clothes, a new bedroom set, a large repair, etc.

EXPENSE WORKSHEET 101

Write down your expenses and total them up at the bottom Name	Total Amount	Type F / V / I / 0	
1 Household Expense	32.92	V	
2 Toiletries	667.57	V	
3 Food	3,204.30	V	
4 Mortgage	9,567.84	F	
5 Electicty / gas	963.58	V	
6 Water & Sewer	283.54	I	
7 Phone / Internet	456.34	V	
9 Home Maintenance	284.71	V	
10 Clothes	1,191.02	O	
11 Education	924.66	V	
12 Other Insurance	1,300.68	I	
13 Health Insurance	3,076.74	F	
14 Furniture	2,100.00	O	
15 Donation	1,278.00	V	
16 Gas	1,764.13	V	
17 Auto Repair	1,531.42	O	
18 Pharmacy	195.19	V	
19 Medical / Dental	149.51	V	
20 Presents / Toys	323.75	O	
21 Travel	461.84	O	
22 Entertainment	612.98	V	
23 Property Tax	6,224.59	I	
24 Federal & State Tax	1,060.80	O	
25 Short term Savings	1,491.00	V	
26 Long term savings	1,491.00	V	
27 Interest / Bank fees	75.00	V	
Total monthly Expenses	40,713.11	-	

Once you have all your expenses labeled as fixed, variable, irregular, or other, carry them over to the appropriate corresponding worksheets. Start by taking your fixed expenses and carry all of them over to Worksheet 102: Fixed Expenses, which is shown below. Add up the monthly expenses (in this case, it'd be for six months). Then divide by the number of months (six) to find and fill in an average Monthly Expense.

WORKSHEET 102: FIXED EXPENSE

Write down your monthly expenses then total them up at the bottom Name	Total Amount	Divide by # of months	Monthly Expense	
1 Mortgage	9,567.84	6	1,594.64	
2 Health Insurance	3,076.74	6	512.79	
Total Expenses	12,644.58	6	2,107.43	

Next, take all your variable expenses, those marked with a "V," and enter them on the Worksheet 103: Variable Expense.

WORKSHEET 103: VARIABLE EXPENSE

Write down your monthly expenses than total them up at the bottom Name	Total Amount	Divide by # of months	Monthly Expense	
1 Household Expense	32.92	6	5.49	
2 Toiletries	667.57	6	111.26	
3 Food	3,204.30	6	534.05	
4 Electicty / gas	963.58	6	160.60	
5 Phone / Internet	456.34	6	76.06	
6 Home Maintenance	284.71	6	47.45	
7 Education	924.66	6	154.11	
8 Donation	1,278.00	6	213.00	
9 Gas	1,764.13	6	294.02	
10 Pharmacy	195.19	6	32.53	
11 Medical / Dental	149.51	6	24.92	
13 Entertainment	612.98	6	102.16	
14 Short term Savings	1,491.00	6	248.50	
15 Long term savings	1,491.00	6	248.50	
16 Interest / Bank fees	75.00	6	12.50	
Total monthly Expenses	13,590.89	6	2,265.15	

Once you have all your variable expenses carried over to Worksheet 103, add up the monthly expenses, and then divide by the number of months of expenses to find an average Monthly Expense.

Using the electric bill from above, your total for six months is $963.58. Divide that total by six (or 963.58/6), which equals $160.59 a month. Your monthly average electric bill will be $160.59, which is what you then enter in the Monthly Expense column. If you have twelve months' worth of expenses, do the same thing, but divide by twelve.

Some expenses, like your electricity bill, will fluctuate throughout the year, depending on the seasons and temperatures. So, if you only track your electricity expenses during the winter, your average will be skewed. That is why the longer time-period you have, the more accurate your average Monthly Expenses will be.

Now that you have carried over your fixed and variable expenses, look back to Worksheet 101. Take all of your irregular expenses ("I") and enter them on Worksheet 104: Irregular Expenses by when you have to pay them (quarterly, every six months, or annually). Divide each irregular expense by the number of months to get the average Monthly Expense, which you'll then enter in the Monthly Expense column.

WORKSHEET 104: IRREGULAR EXPENSES

Write down your monthly expenses then total them up at the bottom Name	Total Amount	Divide by # of months	Monthly Expense	
Every Two Months				
1 Property Tax	6,224.59	6	1,037.43	
Quarterly				
1 Water & Sewer	283.54	6	47.26	
2 Other Insurance	1,300.68	6	216.78	
Total Expenses	7,808.81	6	1,301.47	

As I mentioned earlier, there are things like a yearly vacation or furniture purchased every now and then, which you labeled as "O." Throughout the year, expenses will come up that don't fit anywhere else. Take these expenses and enter them on Worksheet 105: Other Expenses. Take each of your other expenses, divide them by the amount of months of expenses that you have, and carry that average over to your Monthly Expense column.

WORKSHEET 105: OTHER EXPENSES

	Write down your monthly expenses than total them up at the bottom. Name	Total Amount	Divide by # of months	Monthly Expense	
1	Clothes	1,191.02	6	198.50	
2	Furniture	2,100.00	6	350.00	
3	Travel	461.84	6	76.97	
4	Presents / Toys	323.75	6	53.96	
5	Auto repair	1,531.42	6	255.24	
	Fedural & State Tax	1,060.80	6	176.80	
	Total Expenses	6,668.83	6	1,111.47	

Once you have the monthly running average for each expense, carry all monthly expenses over to the appropriate place on the Living Budget Worksheet (shown on the next page). If there is something that you want to do or buy that is outside of your normal budget, find out how much it will cost, divide the amount by twelve, and plug it into your budget. After your budget is completed, enter your monthly Income. Now, add up all the different columns, and then subtract your Total Income from your Total Expenses. The difference is your monthly Net Income or Loss.

Congratulations! You have created your living budget.
Are you ahead or behind?

YOUR LIVING BUDGET

Income	Monthly Amount	Transportation	Monthly Amount
Wages	7,500.00	Gas / Fuel	294.02
Business Income		Insurance	216.78
Interest / Dividends		Repairs	255.24
Total Income	7,500.00	Transportation Totals	766.04
Expenses		Entertainment	
Home		Eating Out / DVD Rentals	102.16
Mortgage / Rent	1,594.64	Movies / Plays	
Utilities	207.86	Concerts / Clubs	
Internet Connection	76.06	Entertainment Totals	102.16
Home / Cellular Telephone			
Home Repairs / Maintenance	47.45	Health	
Furniture	350.00	Health Club Dues	
Property Tax	1,037.43	Health Insurance	512.79
Home Totals	3,313.44	Life / Disability Insurance	
		Medical / Dental	24.92
Daily Living		Prescrip / over the counter	32.53
Groceries	534.05	Health Totals	570.24
Child Care / Education	154.11		
Dry Cleaning / Grooming		Vacations	
House cleaning / supplies	116.75	Plane fare	76.97
Daily Living Totals	804.91	Accoummodations	
		Food	
Financial		Rental Car	
Loan Payments		Vacations Totals	76.97
Credit Card Payments	12.50		
Short term Savings	248.50	Dues / Subscriptions	
Long term Savings	248.50	Magazines / Newspapers	
Federal / State Tax	176.80	Dues / Sub Total	
Financial Totals	686.30		
		Total Income	7,500.00
Personal		Total Expense	6,785.52
Clothing	198.50	Net Income / Loss	714.50
Gifts	53.96		
Charitable Donations	213.00		
Personal Education			
Personal Totals	465.46		

After you have your Living Budget completed, you can determine if your monthly cash flow is either positive or negative, and you can gain a firm grip on your spending and income potential. You are now in a great place to start building a stable financial future. It is at this point that you will be able to really start to become financially free—which is a simple process.

All this process needs is discipline, consistency, and time:

- The **discipline** to create a spending plan and stick to it, no matter how hard it might be
- The **consistency** to follow your plan each and every day
- The **time** to let your investments grow and start to yield your desired results

So that you can see the complete system at a glance, I have it laid out over the next few pages.

A-B-C Your Expenses

Now that you have gotten your Living Budget down on paper, I recommend that now you "A-B-C" your expenses. This will help you prioritize your expenses. When sitting down with clients and helping them A-B-C their expenses, I am often able to help them free up as much as $200 or $300 a month, which can then be used to pay down debt or save and invest for the future. Break down all your expenses into the following:

- **A** expenses are *needs*, such as housing, transportation, food, clothes, etc. These are fixed or variable expenses that you have in order to cover your basic needs.
- **B** expenses are needs that aren't immediately necessary. These expenses are for things that you need or want, but you have control over *when* you get them. B expenses are like a new suit or dress, cable TV, or a new car when the one you have still runs fine.
- **C** expenses are *just* wants or things that you would like to have if you had the money. These are on your wish list.

Step-by-Step Summary

- Step 1: Create a Monthly Expense Log.
- Step 2: Fill out Worksheet 101, then categorize as fixed, variable, irregular, and other expenses (F, V, I, O).
- Step 3: Fill out Worksheet 102: Fixed Expenses.
- Step 4: Fill out Worksheet 103: Variable Expenses.
- Step 5: Fill out Worksheet 104: Irregular Expenses.

- Step 6: Fill out Worksheet 105: Other Expenses.
- Step 7: Complete your Living Budget.

Step one   MONTHLY EXPENSE LOG

EXPENSES							
Household sup.		16.59				16.33	32.92
Toiletries	103.87	298.12	87.22	39.44	92.92	45	666.57
Food	336.22	816.93	482.79	458.87	606.82	502.67	3204.3
Mortgage	1594.64	1594.64	1594.64	1594.64	1594.64	1594.64	9567.84
Electricty / Gas	298.01	181.34	166.97	106.84	101.35	109.07	963.58
Water & Sewer			141.77			141.77	283.54
Phone / Internet	74.87	75.34	79.35	70.34	76.57	79.87	456.34
Clothes	18.96	92.69	301.57	258.87	518.93		1191.02
Education	79.5		364.58	375.23	28.64	76.71	924.66
Other Insurance	70.5		579.84	70.5		579.84	1300.68
Health Insurance	512.79	512.79	512.79	512.79	512.79	512.79	3076.74
Home Maintenance	11.61	175		31.38	66.72		284.71
Furniture		2100					2100
Donation	225	225	225	225	225	225	1350
Gas	281.37	262.35	304.23	337.39	294.3	284.49	1764.13
Auto Rapair	782.2					749.22	1531.42
Pharmacy	43.58	23.22	28.45	34	29.54	36.4	195.19
Medical / Dental	128			21.51			149.51
Presents / toys	50	22.69	30		171.06	50	323.75
Travel	53.31					408.53	461.84
Entertainment	89.35	110	70.79	123.78	89.78	129.28	612.98
Property Tax	3072.21		1576.19			1576.19	6224.59
Fed / State Tax				1060.8			1060.8
Short term savings	262.5	262.5	262.5	262.5	262.5	262.5	1575
Long term savings	262.5	262.5	262.5	262.5	262.5	262.5	1575
Intrest / Bank fee		50		25			75
TOTAL EXP.	8350.99	7081.7	7071.18	5871.38	4934.06	7642.8	40952.11
NET INCOME	-850.99	418.30	428.82	1,628.62	2,565.94	-142.80	4,047.89

Step Two   EXPENSE WORKSHEET 101

Write down your expenses and total them up at the bottom Name	Amount	Type F / V / I / 0	?
1 Household Expense	32.92		
2 Toiletries	667.57		
3 Food	3,204.30		
4 Mortgage	9,567.84		
5 Electicty / gas	963.58		
6 Water & Sewer	283.54		
7 Phone / Internet	456.34		
9 Home Maintenance	284.71		
10 Clothes	1,191.02		
11 Education	924.66		
12 Other Insurance	1,300.68		
13 Health Insurance	3,076.74		
14 Furniture	2,100.00		
15 Donation	1,278.00		
16 Gas	1,764.13		
17 Auto Repair	1,531.42		
18 Pharmacy	195.19		
19 Medical / Dental	149.51		
20 Presents / Toys	323.75		
21 Travel	461.84		
22 Entertainment	612.98		
23 Property Tax	6,224.59		
24 Federal & State Tax	1,060.80		
25 Short term Savings	1,491.00		
26 Long term savings	1,491.00		
27 Interest / Bank fees	75.00		
Total monthly Expenses	**40,713.11**	-	

Step Three FIXED EXPENSE WORKSHEET 102

Write down your monthly expenses then total them up at the bottom Name	Total Amount	Divide by # of months	Monthly Expense	
1 Mortgage	9,567.84	6	1,594.64	
2 Health Insurance	3,076.74	6	512.79	
Total Expenses	12,644.58	6	2,107.43	

Step Four VARIABLE EXPENSE WORKSHEET 103

Write down your monthly expenses than total them up at the bottom Name	Total Amount	Divide by # of months	Monthly Expense	
1 Household Expense	32.92	6	5.49	
2 Toiletries	667.57	6	111.26	
3 Food	3,204.30	6	534.05	
4 Electicty / gas	963.58	6	160.60	
5 Phone / Internet	456.34	6	76.06	
6 Home Maintenance	284.71	6	47.45	
7 Education	924.66	6	154.11	
8 Donation	1,278.00	6	213.00	
9 Gas	1,764.13	6	294.02	
10 Pharmacy	195.19	6	32.53	
11 Medical / Dental	149.51	6	24.92	
13 Entertainment	612.98	6	102.16	
14 Short term Savings	1,491.00	6	248.50	
15 Long term savings	1,491.00	6	248.50	
16 Interest / Bank fees	75.00	6	12.50	
Total monthly Expenses	13,590.89	6	2,265.15	

Step Five   IRREGULAR EXPENSE WORKSHEET 104

Write down your monthly expenses then total them up at the bottom Name	Total Amount	Divide by # of months	Monthly Expense	
Every Two Months				
1 Property Tax	6,224.59	6	1,037.43	
Quarterly				
1 Water & Sewer	283.54	6	47.26	
2 Other Insurance	1,300.68	6	216.78	
Total Expenses	7,808.81	6	1,301.47	

Step Six   OTHER EXPENSE WORKSHEET 105

Write down your monthly expenses than total them up at the bottom. Name	Total Amount	Divide by # of months	Monthly Expense	
1 Clothes	1,191.02	6	198.50	
2 Furniture	2,100.00	6	350.00	
3 Travel	461.84	6	76.97	
4 Presents / Toys	323.75	6	53.96	
5 Auto repair	1,531.42	6	255.24	
Fedural & State Tax	1,060.80	6	176.80	
Total Expenses	6,668.83	6	1,111.47	

Step Seven   YOUR LIVING BUDGET

Income	Amount	Transportation	Amount
Wages	7,500.00	Gas / Fuel	294.02
Business Income		Insurance	216.78
Interest / Dividends		Repairs	255.24
Total Income	**7,500.00**	**Transportation Totals**	**766.04**
Expenses		**Entertainment**	
Home		Eating Out / DVD Rentals	102.16
Mortgage / Rent	1,594.64	Movies / Plays	
Utilities	207.86	Concerts / Clubs	
Internet Connection	76.06	**Entertainment Totals**	**102.16**
Home / Cellular Telephone			
Home Repairs / Maintenance	47.45	**Health**	
Furniture	350.00	Health Club Dues	
Property Tax	1,037.43	Health Insurance	512.79
Home Totals	**3,313.44**	Life / Disability Insurance	
		Medical / Dental	24.92
Daily Living		Prescrip / over the counter	32.53
Groceries	534.05	**Health Totals**	**570.24**
Child Care / Education	154.11		
Dry Cleaning / Grooming		**Vacations**	
House cleaning / supplies	116.75	Plane fare	76.97
Daily Living Totals	**804.91**	Accoummodations	
		Food	
Financial		Rental Car	
Loan Payments		**Vacations Totals**	**76.97**
Credit Card Payments	12.50		
Short term Savings	248.50	**Dues / Subscriptions**	
Long term Savings	248.50	Magazines / Newspapers	
Federal / State Tax	176.80	**Dues / Sub Total**	
Financial Totals	**686.30**		
		Total Income	**7,500.00**
Personal		**Total Expense**	**6,785.52**
Clothing	198.50	**Net Income / Loss**	**714.50**
Gifts	53.96		
Charitable Donations	213.00		
Personal Education			
Personal Totals	**465.46**		

With this example, there is a net income of $714.50 (the last number on the bottom right). You could put that money in your checking account for later or apply it to your emergency fund, if you are in the process of building one. Use this to pay down debt or save/invest for the future. I recommend that you do a combination of all these actions, which I will explain in the next section.

What if your expenses are more than your income?

If your expenses are more than your income, you have three choices: increase your income, reduce your expenses, or do both. Many people use credit cards or lines of credit to cover this difference—and then they wonder why they end up in financial trouble. Whenever you use a debt instrument to balance your budget, it's like being in a hole and trying to dig yourself out from the bottom. The only way to get yourself out of the hole is to stop digging. It's the same way with your finances: until you cut the spillage in your spending and have more money flowing into your budget than out, you will always be playing catch-up.

Once your income exceeds your expenses, you have a surplus that can be plugged into your savings plan. It is at this point that you can really start to get ahead financially. The most important thing now is to stay true to your plan and let the system do its job. All the income you have coming in should be treated equally. As we discussed earlier, when you are self-employed or own a business, you need to use a portion of your net business income to cover your personal salary.

When you get a bonus or make a large sale, don't treat it like normal income and immediately spend it. Apply it straight into your cash flow system. If you do want to buy something with part of it, make sure that you have a predetermined percentage of how much you want to save out of that bonus or sale. Otherwise, it's really easy to spend it all.

It will take about a year to get a good feel for your budget once you begin living according to your spending plan or living budget. If things at times feel out of control, don't worry—that's normal. The most important part of keeping a living budget is monitoring it on a regular basis. Your business and life will change and you will have unexpected expenses throughout the year, so you will need to adjust your budget to meet those changes. Remember, if you don't know how much money is going out, you can't plan for the money that comes in.

The goal of this money management system is to help you create a financial plan that will empower you to take control of your business and finances. All great financial plans start with a systemized living budget and net worth statement...and all great business plans must first start with a solid financial foundation. The system is structured so that all you need to do is move from one page to another.

Congratulations!

You have now completed your living budget and A-B-C-ed your expenses. In the next chapter, I will walk you through the process of creating a net worth statement.

"Many of life's failures are people who did not realize how close they were to success when they gave up."
— Thomas Edison

CHAPTER 15:
DETERMINING YOUR NET WORTH

It's a lot easier to create a net worth/equity statement than a living budget, so you've got a major step behind you. When putting together your net worth/equity statement, you're looking at your assets compared to your liabilities, at one point in time. Many banks require a net worth statement in order to get a loan.

- **Asset:** Something that has value, like a house, a car, jewelry, a business, different investments, or collectables.
- **Liability:** Something which you owe money or have borrowed for, like a mortgage, business loan, car loan, or credit cards. There are short-term and long-term liabilities:
  - Short-term debt or liability: Something you will generally pay off within a year, like a charge you put on your credit card.
  - Long-term debt or liability: A long-term liability is a loan that will take more than a year to pay off, such as a car loan or mortgage.

Just like with the Living Budget process, print out these worksheets on our website, www.entrepreneurshipthatmakescents.com, and fill them in as you go along. I will walk you through the process step-by-step and use examples on the following pages.

- **Step 1: List all your assets on Worksheet 106: Personal Assets.** Once you have all your assets listed, add up their values and put the total on the bottom of the worksheet. Carry that total to the Net Worth/Equity Statement.
- **Step 2: List all your liabilities on Worksheet 107: Personal Liabilities.** Determine if they are short-term or long-term liabilities. Add up their values and carry the total over to the Net Worth/Equity Statement.

Once you have your assets and liabilities listed, do you have a positive net worth or a negative net worth? This is the score card from which you can start to build wealth.

All good financial plans should incorporate a process for paying off debt. In the next section, I will walk you through a step-by-step process for paying off your debt. You will start by paying off your short-term debt and then begin applying the payments toward your long-term debt until you're debt-free. Once you are debt-free, you are able to really begin to grow and accumulate a solid financial foundation.

Now, granted, we have been mostly talking about personal income and expenses and personal assets and liabilities. What does that have to do with growing a business, you ask? Everything! It has everything to do with growing a business. If your personal financial house isn't in order, the stress and expenses will bleed into your business and can cause serious internal hemorrhaging within it. The cash flow management system that I have been talking about for your personal finances is the same concept that you want to adopt into your business.

Remember, cash flow is the lifeline to all small and large businesses. One of my favorite business concepts is creating assets to pay for your liabilities. It's also good to differentiate good debt (things you finance in order to accumulate more income, like a rental house or a business asset) from bad debt (something you finance that depreciates in value and takes away from your income—like a dining room set or new car). Building a business is one of the best ways to create an asset that will pay for liabilities.

Imagine getting up in the morning and knowing that all your current and upcoming expenses are already covered. If you should want to add something new to your personal or business life, instead of acquiring a new liability, all you need to do is move the cash flow hose from one of your existing assets to cover the new liability. And *voilà*, the liability is paid for. What a morning that would be! Now you can walk into your business and truly focus on your passion or dream.

NET WORTH/EQUITY STATEMENT

The reflection of my fortune!

Example:

ASSETS — LIABILITIES = NET WORTH

Assets:

Car	10,000.00
Jewelry	2,000.00
Furniture	7,000.00
House	250,000.00
Total =	**$269,000.00**

Liabilities:

Car Loan	7,000.00
Credit Cards	3,000.00
Line of Credit	15,000.00
Mortgage	170,000.00
Total =	**$195,000.00**
Total Net worth	**$74,000.00**

ASSET WORKSHEET 106

	Name	Amount	
1	House	198,000.00	
2	Car - Camry	8,000.00	
3	Car - Buick	19,450.00	
4	Jewelry	2,500.00	
5	Cash in bank	14,000.00	
6	401 K	127,000.00	
7	Roth IRA	34,359.00	
8	College Fund	17,545.00	
9			
	Total	420,854.00	

LIABILITY WORKSHEET 107

	Name	Type S / L	Balance Owed	
1	Mortgage	L	143,000	
2	Camry Loan	L	4,300	
3	Buick Loan	L	14,500	
4	Credit Cards	S	17,000	
5				
6	Total		178,800	

NET WORTH/EQUITY STATEMENT 108

Personal Financial Profile Assets	Current Value	Liabilities	Balance Owed	
Cash in Banks	14,000.00	Mortgages	143,000.00	
Real Estate Owned	198,000.00	Bank Loans		
Automobiles	27,450.00	Other Loans	18,800.00	
Jewelry	2,500.00	Bank Credit Cards	17,000.00	
Antiques		Bank Credit Cards		
401K	127,000.00	Bank Credit Cards		
Sep IRA / IRA		Bank Credit Cards		
Roth IRA	34,359.00	Dept. Store Cards		
Cash Value Life Insurance		Dept. Store Cards		
Stocks		Alimony / Child Sup		
Bonds		Misc. Liabilities		
Personal Profit Sharing		Misc. Liabilities		
Other Assets - college fund	17,545.00			
Other Assets		Total Liabilities	178,800.00	
Other Assets				
Other Assets		Total assets -	420,854.00	
Other Assets		Total Liabilities	178,800.00	
Total Assets	420,854.00	Net Worth	242,054.00	

Real Estate Owned	Purchase Price	Amount Owed	Current Value	Equity
Your Residence	175,000	143,000.00	198,000.00	55,000.00
Other Real Estate				
Other Real Estate				
Total Real Estate Owned	175,000	143,000.00	198,000.00	55,000.00
Vehicles Owned	25,000.00	4,300.00	8,000.00	3,700.00
Vehicles Owned	22,500.00	14,500.00	19,450.00	4,950.00
Vehicles Owned				
Vehicles Owned				
Total Vehicles Owned	47,500.00	18,800.00	27,450.00	8,650.00

"My problem lies in reconciling my gross habits with my net income."
— Errol Flynn

CHAPTER 16:
CREATING YOUR DEBT-REDUCTION
AND SAVINGS PLAN

Whether in business or life, it's not how much you make—it's how much you save!

Interest on debt grows without rain.
– Yiddish Proverb

One of the largest mistakes entrepreneurs make is they get so caught up in their day-to-day business that they forget about their personal finances. Even though this book is geared toward building a business, for the sake of this exercise, I'm going to focus on your personal financial plan.

I often find that once a client have made all possible cuts in their spending and have their living budget in place, they will still struggle to free up any amount of extra income to put into savings/investments or back into their businesses. So, depending on the amount of disposable income available, I recommend that people begin with "percent bites."

For example, instead of saying people need to save 10% of their available income right away—$100 of every $1,000—I recommend putting a minimum of 3% into their financial management system and living off of 97% of their income. The 3% can then be applied to their savings plan—$30 from $1,000. I then suggest they apply 1% of that $1000 (or $10) to short-term savings, 1% to long-term savings/investing, and 1% to tithing/sharing. The next goal would be to increase the percentages over time.

I am a firm believer in the phrase, "Give it out in slices and it comes back in loaves." When people create a plan for giving back to others (tithing) and start applying that plan, they will often begin to see blessings return in many forms. I have found there is no greater joy than benefiting someone else's life and seeing the impact of that positive influence.

One Christmas, my daughter Sabrina and I decided we were going to collect toys and bring them to a homeless shelter for women and children. The shelter gave us a list of how many toys they needed, plus a few extra. Sabrina and I set out to collect the gifts.

The day before Christmas, we were still a few toys short. It looked like we needed to go to the store and buy the rest. Cash was very tight at the time, and I needed to use the money I had for a limousine lease payment...but we had promised the shelter that we would bring a toy for every child. After praying about the situation, I took a leap of faith. Sabrina and I went shopping and spent $397 on the toys we still needed.

The next morning, we brought the toys to the shelter. It was so gratifying to see the smiles on all those little faces when the gifts were torn open.

The morning after Christmas, a letter showed up in our mailbox. It was from a man I had provided limousine service to three years prior. He had paid with a check that I hadn't been able to cash. I didn't think I would ever see the money again. The letter said, "We are so sorry for taking so long to pay you. We had to move away and didn't have the funds at the time. Things are better now, so here is the money owed for the limousine and a little more. We hope you have a Merry Christmas." Inside the letter was a check for $398!

The following pages will present a step-by-step system for creating a monthly spending, saving, sharing, and debt-reduction plan. It is designed for people at any income level and will walk them through the process of eradicating debt and developing a savings/investment plan. This is the beginning to becoming financially independent.

To better illustrate this monthly savings plan, I'm going to tell you a story of how one couple started to save and invest money, got out of debt, and began the journey to becoming financially independent.

When John and Maryann Smith first began implementing their plan, their monthly take-home income was $4,500. They were spending all they made and were even putting excess expenses on their credit cards.

When I first sat down with them, they told me that they wanted to save money. They knew they were spending more than they should, yet it seemed like there was always "more month at the end of their money." Their purchases included clothes, school supplies for their kids, and entertainment. They often had to put food, insurance, and their utilities on credit cards in order to pay their bills on time. John and Maryann were afraid of losing their jobs— if they did, they wouldn't be able to make ends meet. They were living paycheck-to-paycheck and hated it. It was causing a lot of stress in their marriage, and they weren't able to do the things for their children they wished to.

They didn't think they would ever be able to retire, let alone be able to help their kids pay for college. When they first got married, John's father had told them the Golden Rule of Finance: "Pay yourself ten percent of all that you make." They thought it sounded good but didn't have enough to make ends meet as it was.

We sat and talked for a good couple of hours and they shared their frustrations with me. We talked about their goals, dreams, and what having money meant to them. I then told them they had the ability to achieve their dreams and goals, retire, and even help their children pay for college if they wanted to. However, it would take a lot of work, time, and discipline to make regular deposits into their savings/investment accounts. I could see a sense of peace come over them, and they began to smile again.

The first thing I had them do was put together a budget or spending plan, as we already discussed in Chapter 5.

After going through their expenses, they discovered they could cut some things from their budget and free up extra money. When we got back together, we went through their living budget, and we were able to find even more ways to reduce their monthly expenses/cash outflow.

Insurance

One thing assessed was their insurance policies. It turned out they had really low deductibles. I explained that many people carry low deductibles because they are afraid of the potential out-of-pocket costs in emergencies. The lower the deductible, the higher the insurance premium. Plus, if unforeseen things do happen, don't call the 1-800 help desk or anyone except your personal insurance agent about filing a claim. They will have to file a claim on your insurance record, even if you decide not to file a claim.

Like most people, however, the Smiths didn't know that even if they had an accident or something happened to their house, their monthly premium could be hit with a 10% (or higher) surcharge that would remain on their policy for up to three years. Plus, insurance companies have a score, like a credit score, which will affect the cost of one's insurance—or even determine if they are able to get insurance at all.

This means that filing a claim for anything less than one thousand dollars could often cost more than they would get from the insurance company. I explained that they would be better off self-insuring the first thousand dollars and use their insurance for large claims. A great way to accomplish that is to create an **insurance savings account** and fund it over time until it has a thousand dollars in it.

The Smiths liked that idea, so I had them call their agent and raise the deductible to a thousand dollars, which reduced their insurance premiums by $30 a month.

Tax Refunds

The Smiths told me they always got a tax refund at the end of the year for around $2,000. I had John tell the personnel director or HR person where he worked to increase the number of exemptions he put down to reduce the amount of money taken out of his paycheck every month. John would have a smaller tax refund at the end of the year, but the family would have more money to use each month. The goal of your paid-in tax is to ensure you don't have a tax bill at the end of the year—but you don't want to pay too much in, either.

Eating Out
We also found that John was eating out three to four times a week, so he agreed to pack a lunch instead and only eat out from time to time.

Phone/Cable Plan
I also had John call his phone/cable company to negotiate a less expensive plan. Cable companies are always competing with each other, so if you call them and threaten to switch to one of their competitors, they will often give you a better deal in order to keep you as a customer.

By the time we were done with the first series of cuts, the Smiths had reduced their expenses to only 97% of their income.

Creating an Emergency Fund
We then talked about how they felt financially insecure because they didn't have an emergency fund in place. Whenever something happened, they would whip out their credit cards to cover it, therefore increasing their debt load.

I explained that the challenge with not having an emergency fund was that if they didn't have any money set aside for emergencies, life would at times seem like a string of emergencies. I then recommended that an emergency fund be the first area they build up. I told them to accumulate enough savings to cover at least three months—ideally six months—of their current monthly living expenses.

I've found that if people don't have at least three months of living expenses set aside in an emergency fund, they are continually playing catch-up. Or, as I like to say, referring back to Murphy's Law: "If you invite Murphy, he won't show up. But when you're not ready, he is sure to come."

John and Maryann started putting any extra money into their emergency fund and then went to work on reducing their short-term debt. After going through John and Maryann's debts, I suggested they start to save money and pay down their debt at the same time.

It is important to apply money toward both debt reduction and savings at the same time. I find that many people will either save money or pay down their debt—however, they need to go hand-in-hand.

By staying true to their plan, the Smiths became disciplined in saving money and began the journey to reaching financial freedom—their savings began to grow, and their debt began to disappear.

Liquid Assets

The next time we got together, I told them a good goal would be having at least one year of expenses in various accounts, easily accessible or liquid, just in case something happened. There is nothing better than knowing you could go a year without any income and you'd financially survive.

Some options for placing savings are:

- Three months of expenses in a passbook savings or money market account for emergencies
- Three months of expenses in an account or investments that yield a better return, are safe from potential risk, and are very conservative

Once John and Maryann had their emergency funds in place, were paying themselves first every time they got paid, and were consistently applying money toward expenses, short-term/midterm/long-term savings, and charity, I recommended that they start to increase the percentages.

John, Maryann, and I met two weeks later to fine-tune their plan and to discuss their progress. They were coming along wonderfully and staying disciplined with their plan. So, I recommended they keep working on reducing their expenses, and we set a goal to get their living expenses down to 90% of their income within the next three months.

For some people, getting expenses down to 90% of their income can take one or two months. It might take others as long as six months. I would recommend, however, that you try to reach the point where you are living on 90% of your income within the first three months of implementing this money-management system.

John and Maryann were starting to feel more comfortable with this system. I recommend that they start to build up the percentages they applied for charity/tithing to 10% as quickly as possible. They would feel good being able to help others.

I expressed how helping others increases self-confidence dramatically. It is from the process of applying systems and having the discipline to develop a strong savings plan that we are able to start developing a wealth-oriented mindset.

After two-and-a-half months, John and Maryann were living on only 90% of their income and applying 10% to their money-management system. We got back together for a progress check, and I even brought them a cake to celebrate their accomplishments.

After we celebrated, I said a good mid- to long-term goal would be increasing their savings/investing and sharing to the point that they were living on only 70% of what they made and applying 30% to their plan. For most people, depending on where they are financially, this may take a while. That's okay—it's a mid- to long-term goal.

After going back through their budget and expenses, Maryann told me that she'd always wanted to start a small business. She even had a friend with a small e-commerce business. Her friend had told Maryann that she would help her start one if she wanted, too. Maryann asked me if I thought that was a good idea. I told her to do more research about the business idea and put together a plan. We would get back together in a week and I would review it for her.

I continued meeting with John and Maryann once a quarter to make sure they were staying on track. It took some time, but they reached the point where they were living on only

70% of what they made and saving, sharing, and investing the rest. They had set the goal, and they finally made it.

Maryann called me and said, "We did it, we did it! We finally reached our goal. We are now able to put 30% of what we make back into our financial plan."

"That's fantastic, Maryann," I said. "I knew you two would get there. How does it feel?"

"It feels amazing. John and I now know that we will be able to reach other goals we have. In fact, we can't wait until we are able to check off becoming debt-free, as well," Maryann said, giggling.

"Well, Maryann, you just made my day. I would like to take you and John out for dinner to celebrate. How does next Friday look for you two?"

"Friday looks great," Maryann responded.

Friday evening came, and we had a wonderful dinner. After dinner, while we were eating dessert, we went back over their goals and again discussed their beliefs about money. I suggested that, since they were now living on only 70% of what they made, they then allocate 10% to charity, 10% to short-term, more conservative savings/investments, and 10% to mid- or long-range retirement investing.

I explained that the degree of aggressiveness in which they invest in the long-term depended on their age and risk tolerance. There are many components that go into any investment mix, and any investments should ideally be reviewed at least quarterly—and if not quarterly, every six months to a year at the bare minimum.

It is important to develop a working relationship with a good financial advisor—one who has the experience to deal with many different situations, yet is able to have a holistic or comprehensive approach. An advisor should be able to put his or her clients' needs first, yet have access to a wide range of solutions.

I told John and Maryann how important it was to have an advisor with a long-term perspective to help them create and stay on track with their financial plan. Their advisor should sit down with them to create a list of goals, help them stay on track, continue to monitor their current situation, and determine the best course of action to take according to their goals.

Maryann said, smiling, "We know, Mike. That is why we are so thankful for having you in our corner. You have helped make the process of saving money, getting out of debt, and investing for the future so much easier. Thanks to all your help, we now know that we will be all right financially."

"Thank you, John and Maryann. I know that you have been working on your money-management system for a while now. You've been making great progress," I responded, smiling.

Two Different Scenarios for Building Net Worth

I am now going to walk you through two different scenarios: one without short-term debt, and one with short-term debt. We are going to use John and Maryann's situation as an example to show you how the process works. Both scenarios start with a monthly combined take-home pay of $4,500. Both will be living on 97% of that take-home pay and allocating 1% to sharing/tithing, 1% to short-term savings, and 1% to long-term savings.

Scenario #1 (no short-term debt):

$4,500 = Take-home pay
97% = $4,365 to cover living expenses
1% = $45 to charity
1% = $45 to short-term savings
1% = $45 to long-term savings/investments

Short-term savings tend to be more liquid, or easily converted into needed cash. Long-term savings are those that go toward investments with terms over one year.

As I discussed earlier, if you don't have an emergency fund, I recommend that the first thing you do is to build up that fund to cover all your expenses for three to six months. Until you get your emergency fund in place and funded, the amount you would normally apply to short-term savings and long-term investing should be put into your emergency fund. In our example, that would be $13,095 ($4,365 x 3 months), or better yet, six months: $26,190 ($4,365 x 6 months).

If your monthly expenses go up or down, I recommend that you adjust your emergency fund accordingly. Let's say that your monthly expenses were $3,800 instead of $4,365...then you would only need $11,400 ($3,800 x 3 months) to $22,800 ($3,800 x 6 months) in your emergency fund.

If your monthly outgoing expenses are $4,365 and you apply 1% toward charity/tithing and 2% to short- and long-term savings, at the end of three months, your accounts should look like this:

Money set aside for charity: $45 x 3 = $135
Money set aside for savings: $90 x 3 = $270

After working this system for three months, let's assume that you have your budget in place and are spending only 90% of what you make. You are now able to apply 10% to your savings plan. At this point, I recommend that you decide how you want to build up the amount you share/tithe until you reach 10%.

Because it's so important to have your emergency fund in place, I recommend that you raise the amount you apply to sharing/tithing equally to the other two parts: 3% charity, 3.5% short-term savings, and 3.5% long-term savings.

This is what it would look like:

$4,500 = Monthly take-home pay
90% = $4,050 for living expenses
10% of $4,500 = $450 to charity/tithing and savings
3% = $135 to charity
3.5% = $157.50 to short-term savings
3.5% = $157.50 to long-term savings/investments

At the end of nine months, your savings should look like this:

Money set aside for charity:
Months 1 to 3: $45 x 3 = $135
Months 4 to 12: $135 x 9 = $1,215
Total at the end of nine months:
$135 + 1,215 = $1,350

Money set aside for savings:
Months 1 to 3: $90 x 3 = $270
Months 4 to 12: $157.50 x 9 = $1,417.50
Total at the end of nine months:
$270 + $1,417.50 = $1,552.50

Scenario #2 (with short-term debt):

So, what happens if you have short-term debt? These are debts that you would normally pay off within one year, such as credit card debt. In this case, split the amount you are putting into savings and pay one-half toward short-term savings and half toward paying off your short-term debt instead of placing this money into long-term savings/investing.

Again, let's look at John and Maryann's situation. When they first started, they did not have an emergency fund. We therefore set a goal of creating a fund that would cover six months of their living expenses. John and Maryann also owed $13,500 in credit card debt and had a car loan of $8,500, which equaled a combined debt balance of $22,000. They set a goal to pay off that debt in five years. Given their financial situation, we recommended applying their percentages like so:

$4,500 = Combined take-home pay
97% = $4,365 to cover living expenses
1% = $45 to charity
1% = $45 to short-term savings
1% = $45 to paying off short-term debt

Depending on your debt-load and personal belief system, you decide how quickly or slowly you increase the amount you put toward sharing or tithing. For the purpose of this exercise, however, we are going to keep the numbers the same as in Scenario #1.

After three months, the numbers would look like this:

$45 x 3 = $135 to charity/tithing
$45 x 3 = $135 to short-term savings
$45 x 3 = $135 to short-term debt reduction

Continue using this formula until your short-term debt is paid off.

To continue illustrating this system, we'll follow John and Maryann Smith's progress over the course of one year. As in Scenario #1, after three months, John and Maryann were able to reduce their monthly expenses to 90% of their take-home pay, allowing them to apply 30% to charity, 3.5% to short-term savings—and this time, 3.5% to short-term debt reduction.

Money set aside for **charity/tithing**:
Months 1 to 3: $45 x 3 = $135
Months 4 to 12: $135 x 9 = $1,215
Total at the end of 12 months:
    $135 + $1,215 = $1,350

Money set aside for **short-term savings**:
Months 1 to 3: $45 x 3 = $135
Months 4 to 12: $157.50 x 9 = $1,417.50
Total at the end of 12 months:
    $135 + $1,417.50 = $1,552.50

Money put toward **short-term debt reduction**:
Months 1 to 3: $45 x 3 = $135
Months 4 to 12: $157.50 x 9 = $1,417.50
Total at the end of 12 months:
    $135 + $1,417.50 = $1,552.50

By the beginning of year two, John and Maryann were bringing home $4,700 a month and living on 80% of their income, or $3,760. Of the remaining 20%, they decided to increase the percentage given to charity to 6% ($282) and short-term savings to 7% ($329) of their take-home pay. They also increased the percentage that went to debt-reduction or long-term savings/investment to 7% ($329), as well.

$4,700 combined take-home pay
80% for living expenses: $3,760

20% to distribute to charity, short-term savings/emergency fund, and debt reduction:
6% to charity/tithing: $282
7% to short-term savings: $329
7% to debt reduction/long-term savings: $329

I recommended that the Smiths continue to apply $329 to reducing their short-term debt until it was completely paid off.

After that, the 7% could be applied to long-term savings or investments.

At the end of 24 months, the Smith's savings plan looked like this:

Money set aside for **charity/tithing**:
Months 1 to 3: $45 x 3 = $135
Months 4 to 12: $135 x 9 = $1,215
Months 13 to 24: $282 x 12 = $3,384
Total at the end of 24 months:
$135 + $1,215 + 3,384 = $4,734

Money set aside for **short-term savings/emergency fund**:
Months 1 to 3: $45 x 3 = $135
Months 4 to 12: $157.50 x 9 = $1,417.50
Months 13 to 24: $329 x 12 = $3,948
Total at the end of 24 months:
$135 + $1,417.50 + $3,948 = $5,500.50

Money put toward **short-term debt reduction**:
Months 1 to 3: $45 x 3 = $135
Months 4 to 12: $157.50 x 9 = $1,417.50
Months 13 to 24: $329 x 12 = $3,948
Total at the end of 24 months:
    $135 + $1,417.50 + $3,948 = $5,500.50

Going into year three, the Smiths were earning $4,900 combined per month and living on only 70% of their income, or $3,430. Then they were able to increase the amount they donated to charitable causes to 10% ($490), 10% ($490) to short-term savings, and 10% ($490) to debt reduction or long-term savings/investments per month.

Even though they were making more money per month, the Smiths were able to reduce their monthly living expenses by following their monthly savings plan. This also meant that they could reduce the amount of money in their emergency fund from $13,095 (3 months x $4,365) to $10,290...or $26,190 (6 months x $4,365) to $20,540. As you can see, you can speed up your wealth-accumulation process by either reducing your expenses, increasing your income, or doing both.

Now the Smith's savings looked like this:

Money set aside for **charity/tithing**:
Months 1 to 3: $45 x 3 = $135
Months 4 to 12: $135 x 9 = $1,215
Months 13 to 24: $282 x 12 = $3,384
Months 25 to 36: $490 x 12 = $5,880
Total at the end of 36 months:
        $135 + $1,215 + 3,384 + $5,880 = $10,614

Money set aside for **short-term savings/emergency fund**:
Months 1 to 3: $45 x 3 = $135
Months 4 to 12: $157.50 x 9 = $1,417.50
Months 13 to 24: $329 x 12 = $3,948
Months 25 to 36: $490 x 12 = $5,880

Total at the end of 36 months:
    $135 + $1,417.50 + $3,948 + $5,880 = $11,380.50

Money set aside for **debt reduction/long-term savings**:
Months 1 to 3: $45 x 3 = $135
Months 4 to 12: $157.50 x 9 = $1,417.50
Months 13 to 24: $329 x 12 = $3,948
Months 25 to 36: $490 x 12 = $5,880
Total at the end of 36 months:
    $135 + $1,417.50 + $3,948 + $5,880 = $11,380.50

In year four, Maryann's boss was so happy with her work that he gave her a raise and a yearend bonus of $5,000. The Smith's take-home pay was now $5,200 a month. They continued living on 70% of their take-home pay ($3,640) and set aside 10% ($520) for donations, short-term savings, debt reduction, and long-term investments.

John and Maryann remembered our conversation about filling their emergency fund before doing anything else. They also recalled that following their monthly savings plan would take time, discipline, and hard work. As long as they stayed faithful to their plan, I recommended that they celebrate their successes by taking a small amount out of their budget to acknowledge their achievements. It's important to acknowledge and celebrate successes to stay motivated.

Over a romantic dinner at a nice restaurant, John and Maryann decided to use $500 (10% of the $5,000 bonus) to take a short trip with their kids. They would then put the rest of the bonus into their emergency fund. The Smith's dedication and commitment paid off. At the end of year four, to summarize, John and Maryann's savings looked like this:

Money set aside for **charity/tithing**:
Months 1 to 3: $45 x 3 = $135
Months 4 to 12: $135 x 9 = $1,215
Months 13 to 24: $282 x 12 = $3,384
Months 25 to 36: $490 x 12 = $5,880

Months 37 to 48: $520 x 12 = $6,240
Total at the end of 48 months:
    $135 + $1,215 + 3,384 + $5,880 + $6,240 = $16,854

Money set aside for **short-term savings/emergency fund**:
Months 1 to 3: $45 x 3 = $135
Months 4 to 12: $157.50 x 9 = $1,417.50
Months 13 to 24: $329 x 12 = $3,948
Months 25 to 36: $490 x 12 = $5,880
Months 37 to 48: $520 x 12 = $6,240
Plus the remainder of Maryann's bonus: $4,500
Total at the end of 48 months:
    $135 + $1,417.50 + $3,948 + $5,880 + $6,240 + $4,500 =
                    $22,120.50

Money set aside for **debt reduction/long-term savings:**
Months 1 to 3: $45 x 3 = $135
Months 4 to 12: $157.50 x 9 = $1,417.50
Months 13 to 24: $329 x 12 = $3,948
Months 25 to 36: $490 x 12 = $5,880
Months 37 to 48: $520 x 12 = $6,240
Total at the end of 48 months:
    $135 + $1,417.50 + 3,948 + $5,880 + $6,240 = $17,620

One day, my phone rang—it was Maryann again.
"Mike, we did it! We did it!" I could hear her excitement over the phone.
"What did you do?" I asked.
"We finally fully funded our emergency fund, and we have money left over. Right now, we are only spending $3,640 a month and have $22,120 in our short-term savings account. That's enough to cover six months of our living expenses!" she explained.
"Wow, that's great! You and John should be very proud. How's your debt reduction coming along?"
"We have paid our short-term debt down by $17,620.50 and only have $4,379.50 left to go," she told me, still excited.

"Wonderful, Maryann. You two will have that paid down in no time," I said.

"I know. I can't wait. It feels like we have been paying things off forever," she said.

"Remember, I told you and John when we first met that this would take time. You two are doing really well. I'm proud of you for sticking to your savings plan. Keep up the great work!"

The Smiths continued their debt-reduction plan with the goal of being debt-free (except for their mortgage) within five years, as previously stated. They discussed how they had been able to pay off all of their credit card debt then roll those payments into their car loan. They paid the car loan off nine months into year five, which allowed them to reach their goal. After meeting with them, we went out to lunch to celebrate.

Time, Patience, and Perseverance

As you can see from John and Maryann's story, it can take a while to build an emergency fund, pay off short-term debt, and move into long-term saving and/or investing. It took the Smiths four years to save up six months of living expenses in their emergency fund and five years to pay off all their short-term debt. How quickly you are able to get control of your financial future depends on how much you can reduce your expenses and/or how quickly you can increase your income.

Building up savings takes time, so you need to remain patient through the process. The extent to which you can reduce your expenses can be challenging. One main benefit of owning a business is that it gives you more control over the amount of income you're able to make. Whereas if you are employed, the degree to which you can increase your take-home pay may be limited.

If you do still have a job, set a goal for when you want to move full-time into your business. You have probably heard the phrase, "Don't quit your day job." This only holds true until your personal business or investments reach the point where they bring in more money than your job does. This does not mean you should look for get-rich-quick schemes. Know that building your business or investments to the point of being able to live on the interest takes time.

Remember that you're in control of how quickly your savings grow. The road to financial independence is paved with time, discipline, and continually funding your financial plan month after month. Hang in there!

"Money is a terrible master, but an excellent servant."

— P.T. Barnum

"We first make our habits, and then our habits make us."

— John Dryden

CHAPTER 17:
BECOMING DEBT-FREE

To create wealth, separate your bad debt from good debt, then eliminate your bad debt!

This chapter offers a great system for reducing or paying down short-term debt. Some people will pay off their credit card or a short-term loan and then put the "extra" money back into their budget to spend. They then end up spending their newly freed-up money instead of using it to continue paying down their debt or applying it to their saving/investing plan.

People often ask me, "If I start applying a percentage of what I am making to paying down my debt, what do I pay off first?" or, "Do I just pay the minimum payments?" or, "When I pay off this credit card, do I just cut it up?" There are many answers to these questions and what follows will provide some guidelines for reducing and eliminating your debt.

Eliminating Your Debt

The trick to paying off debt is making your progress fun and easy to follow *consistently*. You will pick up momentum as you start to pay off one credit card, then the next, and the next.

The system works like this: First, organize your short-term debt in order of amount owed, from the lowest to the highest balance. Some financial advisors recommend ranking your short-term debts from the highest interest rates to the lowest. That makes sense because you'd be reducing the amount of interest you pay, but I'll show you a different way to look at reducing debts.

If you have four credit cards and the card with the highest interest rate has the highest balance, you will be paying toward the card for a long time, and it won't feel like you're getting anywhere. However, if you rank the cards by the lowest balance amount first, you will be able to pay the first card off sooner, which will give you a great sense of accomplishment. You will then transfer the payment from the first card to the card with the next lowest balance. Simply follow the process to the next card and the next until they're all paid off.

The Debt Snowball:
Once you start to pay off your debt, you begin to create forward momentum toward financial independence. Your net worth will quickly increase and your debt will quickly begin to disappear.

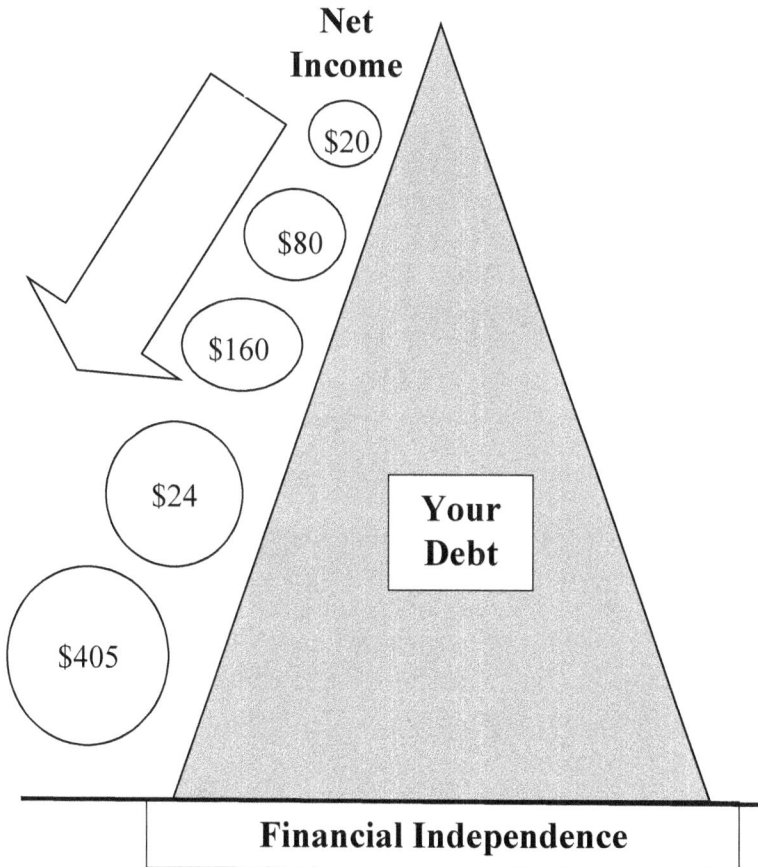

Net Income

$20

$80

$160

$24

$405

Your Debt

Financial Independence

Once your credit cards are paid off, transfer the amount you were paying toward the cards to any longer- or midterm debt you may have, such as a car loan. Once the car loan is paid off, then apply the payments toward other long-term debt or your mortgage. This system is referred to as the "debt snowball." While the "snowball" might start at a very low amount, like your "minimum payment," it will pick up size as it rolls down the hill.

Here's what that looks like with the numbers:

- **Visa 1:** 18% interest; you owe $3,000; minimum payment is $80
- **Visa 2:** 14% interest; you owe $4,500; minimum payment is $160
- **MasterCard:** 17% interest; you owe $6,000; minimum payment is $165

Pay $80 until the first card is paid off, then start paying the $80 plus the minimum payment on Visa 2:

$$\$80 + \$160 = \$240$$

Once the second card is paid off, you move the $240 to the third card:

$$\$240 + \$165 = \$405$$

Once the third card is paid off, you apply the $405 to paying off long-term debt.

When you begin this process, continue to pay at least the minimum due on each card every month, then try to pay more toward the card with the lowest balance when you can. Once you have paid off that card, you will have a great feeling of accomplishment. To better illustrate, look at the chart on the next page.

Visa 1	Visa 2	Master Card
18% Interest; Balance of $3,000; Minimum Payment $80	14% Interest; Balance of $4,500; Minimum Payment $160	17% Interest; Balance of $6,000; Minimum Payment $165
Pay off the first card, then move the $80 to the second card.	$ 80 $160 $240 Once the second card is paid off, then apply the $240.00 to the third card.	$240 $165 $405 Once the third card is paid off, move the $405 to other mid or long-term debt.

Now let's look at paying back midterm debt. Say there is a car loan for $350 with a balance of $8,500.

> Loan balance: $8,500
> Monthly loan payment: $350
> Amount now available because credit cards are now paid off: $405...OR $405 + $385 = $755

Use the $755.00 to pay off your car loan. Then move the $735.00 to the next loan until all short-term, midterm, and long-term debts are paid off.

Once you're able to start applying extra money toward your financial management system, you will really start to see your wealth begin to grow. As you can see, by transferring the payments from one card to another, you will begin to pick up momentum—and before you know it, your debt will be paid off. Then, once your debt is paid off, if you transfer the debt payments into your savings/investing plan, your wealth creation will begin to really take off.

You have now paid off all your debt except for your mortgage. Some common questions I'm often asked are, "Should I apply the money I have been paying toward my debt to paying my mortgage off early?" or, "Should I apply the money I've been paying toward debt to my retirement/wealth accumulation plan?" I believe you need to do both. Once your short-term and midterm debt is gone, I recommend that you apply as much as you comfortably can toward your long-term retirement/wealth accumulation plan.

The real question is how quickly you should pay off your mortgage. Some people feel they are more comfortable paying off their mortgage early. For many people, owning their house completely free and clear brings with it a great peace of mind. However, paying off your mortgage early doesn't always make the most financial sense.

On the surface, paying off your mortgage early sounds great—if you have enough money coming in each month to still fund your retirement. If you pay more toward your mortgage, you may not have enough extra to invest toward retirement. Owning your house free of debt makes it your largest financial asset, but you may not be able to access the money if you ever needed to. I refer to this as being "land rich and cash poor." This could be a bad place to be if you want to keep living in your house into retirement.

If the interest rate on your mortgage is very low, you may be able to find a better place to invest your money. This is referred to as **opportunity cost**, or the cost of choosing one thing over another. Another risk in making extra mortgage payments is that if you were to lose your job and needed to access the equity in your house, you probably wouldn't be able to. Without a job, the bank won't give you a loan, even if you have already paid off most of the mortgage and you only owe a small amount. In addition, if for some reason you're unable to make the mortgage payments, you could risk going into foreclosure.

With all of that said, there is a great trick for paying off your mortgage early—and only paying a little bit more than you would have to otherwise. Instead of paying your mortgage once a month as you normally would, make your mortgage payment every two weeks. This is done by telling your lender that you want to make biweekly payments, or half the mortgage in the first two weeks and half the mortgage payment two weeks later. That way, you end up making one extra payment each year, which will allow you to pay off your mortgage in twenty-three years instead of thirty.

Another approach is, rather than making extra payments on your mortgage, investing the money in a very conservative long-term savings/investment account that yields more interest than you're paying on your mortgage. This money would be liquid (more readily available). This way, your money would grow quicker than it would if you were paying off the mortgage. Plus, you would remain in control of the money. As the long-term savings/investment account grows, you would be able to withdraw money from that account and pay off your mortgage if you chose to.

When it comes to deciding if you should pay your mortgage off early instead of applying available cash flow to your retirement or wealth-creation plan, there are many different variables within your overall financial picture. I therefore highly recommend you take a close look at your goals, your current financial condition, and your overall financial plan. Then, after discussing your plan with your financial advisor, decide which method is the best fit for what you're trying to accomplish and which option best fits your financial situation and risk comfort level.

Remember, there are two kinds of debt: good debt and bad debt. Good debt is when you borrow money to acquire an asset that helps you earn more money, such as an investment into your business. For instance, I borrowed $50,000 to purchase a limousine. My monthly payments were $1,500, but the limousine brought in $5,000 in income per month. Without borrowing the money, I wouldn't have been able to buy the limousine, and therefore I couldn't have earned the $3,500. On the other hand, an example of bad debt would be running up $10,000 on a credit card to buy things that you can't use to produce more revenue or income with.

As I mentioned before, when you truly put a system in place for creating wealth, the most important component of that system is the consistency with which you put the various steps into place, coupled with the discipline of following them every day.

Even something as small as consistently adding $1 to your savings/investment plan over time will turn into a fortune if it's done each and every day. When you consistently divide your income up into the three parts (spending, saving, and sharing), your financial state will improve. Unfortunately, most people are too busy looking for ways to make a lot of money and miss out on the little things that will turn into a fortune over time.

As Jim Rohn says, "Wealth is created from our savings, not our earnings."

Let's illustrate with a story about Mr. Smith, an old farmer who always dreamed of finding a large diamond. He would feed his animals and quickly plow his fields. He went around the countryside looking for diamonds every day until he got frustrated and quit farming. Mr. Smith sold his farm and went out searching for diamonds. He scoured diamond mine after diamond mine until he was too old to dig.

One morning, Mr. Smith picked up a newspaper and saw an article about a guy who discovered the largest diamond ever found. To Mr. Smith's surprise, the gentleman found the diamond while he was plowing his field, preparing to plant his spring crops. He was the very same gentleman who bought Mr. Smith's farm. Mr. Smith had gone out searching for diamonds, yet he had lived right on top of the largest diamond around and never saw it because he was too busy looking in other places. Like Mr. Smith, many people say they want to become a millionaires or make a lot of money, yet they will move from one get-rich-quick idea to another...or they will spend their weekly or monthly salary as soon as it comes in, whether it's $500 or $10,000, leaving nothing saved for later. That is where they run in trouble.

A great way to earn more income, grow your business, or increase your current salary is to find something and leave it better than you found it. You can also help people solve their problems. It could be a product or service. Look around and find something that's broken and fix it, or find a service that could be done better and improve upon it. If you continue to give back to society and bring in new and improved products and services, your own value will improve—then keep tabs on your money.

In my own business, I should've known that we were headed toward financial trouble when my wife asked me how much money we were spending, and I answered, "I'm not sure. Not much." The scary part was that I thought I had a pretty good handle on our finances. It wasn't until I finally sat down and did a living budget that I realized we were actually upside down and didn't know it.

As I discussed in Chapter 3, it's very important that while you begin to build a strong financial foundation, you also need to grow yourself personally. There are different levels you will need to move through. And if you skip any of those levels, your foundation will not be as strong. It makes no sense to build a beautiful house if the foundation is made of sand.

I began this section by having you create a living budget and talked about why it's important to plan your expenses around your lifestyle. I showed you some great ways to purge your expenses so you are able to free up extra cash flow that can be invested. I also explained the importance of having an emergency fund. Then you created a net worth statement and listed all your assets and liabilities.

Once you created a living budget and net worth statement and you knew what your net worth was, I walked you through a detailed process for paying off your short-term, midterm, and long-term debt. I also talked about whether or not it makes sense to pay your mortgage off early. Now comes the fun part: wealth creation.

By now, you're able to consistently invest money into your business or financial plan. If you haven't yet, now is the time you may want to sit down with a financial professional or an investment advisor and put together a comprehensive financial plan.

When you design your plan, it's very important that you create a one that works around your lifestyle. As things in your life change, you will want to make the necessary adjustments to your plan. There are many different rules and limitations that apply to different investments, so please contact your financial advisor or tax professional for the most current strategies or programs.

When setting up your retirement plan, it's very important to set a goal to fully fund the maximum amount possible. With that said, it's better to start by funding less and doing it more often. As it is with everything else, the more consistent you are with your saving/investing, the easier it will become.

Again, congratulations! You made it through the hardest part of the book: getting your own financial house in order. If I learned nothing else through my journey of raising three children and learning about money and business at the same time, at least I learned that a good understanding of my own finances makes it easier to design, build, and grow a business. That is why I put this part in the middle of the book.

The great part of this money-management system is that it works for any age. Unlike my adult clients, I teach kids to get used to only spending 50%, saving 40%, and sharing 10% of the money they get. The goal with this system is for people to get used to only spending a percent of what they make so that, as their income begins to grow, they have already developed the habit of saving a large portion. People need to learn that when they get a dollar, they can't spend the whole dollar—and they will be better at managing their money.

In workshops, I like to ask the question, "If I were to write you a check for a hundred thousand dollars, would you want it all now? Or would you want a penny now, and have it double each day for thirty days?" Most will go for the hundred thousand dollar check immediately. Which would you choose? Now take a look at this chart. Did you make the right decision?

Day 1	$ 0.01	Day 16	$ 377.68
Day 2	$ 0.02	Day 17	$ 655.36
Day 3	$ 0.04	Day 18	$ 1,310.72
Day 4	$ 0.08	Day 19	$ 2,621.44
Day 5	$ 0.16	Day 20	$ 5,242.88
Day 6	$ 0.32	Day 21	$ 10,485.76
Day 7	$ 0.64	Day 22	$ 20,971.52
Day 8	$ 1.28	Day 23	$ 41,943.04
Day 9	$ 2.56	Day 24	$ 83,886.08
Day 10	$ 5.12	Day 25	$ 167,772.16
Day 11	$ 10.24	Day 26	$ 335,544.32
Day 12	$ 20.48	Day 27	$ 671,088.64
Day 13	$ 40.96	Day 28	$ 1,342,177.28
Day 14	$ 81.92	Day 29	$ 2,684,354.56
Day 15	$ 163.84	Day 30	$ 5,368,709.12

Albert Einstein talked about the eighth wonder of the world: compound interest. Granted, in real life, money doesn't generally double every day. But it illustrates the point.

That said, as the Rule of 72 points out, money will double at the rate of dividing the return on your money. Take 6% by 72, and that will tell you how long it will take for it to double. This is how it works: divide the number 72 by a specific rate of return on your money, and it will show you how long it will take for your money to double. People often say that they need more money, but as you can see, it's not the amount you have invested; rather, it's the return you get on the amount invested that really makes the difference, as the chart on the next page will demonstrate.

Let's say you invest $10,000 between ages 29 and 65 and you get the following returns:

4%	Age	8%	Age	12%	Age
$10,000	29	$10,000	29	$10,000	29
$20,000	47	$20,000	38	$20,000	35
$40,000	65	$40,000	47	$40,000	41
$80,000		$80,000	56	$80,000	47
$160,000		$160,000	65	$160,000	53
				$320,000	59
				$640,000	65

As the chart demonstrates, the difference between 4% and 12% yields $640.00 versus $40,000 at age 65—that's a difference of $600,000.

This is why I always say that all fortunes begin with a sound plan and the discipline to stay on track!

"Compound interest is the eighth wonder of the world. He who understands it, earns it. He who doesn't, pays it."

— Albert Einstein

CHAPTER 18:
PROTECTING YOUR NET WORTH

Building a business without the proper protection is like building a house on sand!

It's important to keep an even balance between safety and business. In this chapter, I will talk about ways to protect your assets. As with any business expense, it's important not to spend too much on insurance, but it is critical that you have adequate coverage for your business and yourself. As a businessperson, you're exposed to more risks. A great visual for illustrating the importance of proper business and personal coverage is the building of a house.

The first thing you create when you start to build a house is a plan. Perhaps it's an architect's drawing or blueprint showing what your house is going to look like. Then you lay the foundation. The foundation of a house is similar to your business and financial plans, which is why it's so important that they be comprehensive, even if you're just starting out. The more detailed the plans, the stronger the foundation will be.

Next, you frame the outside of the house. You need to choose the materials that will best suit your house while providing stability and beauty. This would be the equivalent of establishing your timeline, short-term, midterm, and long-term goals, and selecting the best vehicles or strategies to accomplish those goals.

After your house is framed and your exterior walls are in place, you build the roof so that you can protect them from damaging elements. This is equivalent to creating a financial plan with proper protection (insurance) to safeguard you from unforeseen catastrophes.

The final steps in building your house are lying out rooms and adding finishing touches. For your financial house, that would mean putting your current assets into the plan and deciding which future assets will go where.

If you build a house with a solid foundation and follow the proper steps while building it, that house will stand strongly and become a safe environment for you and your family. If you design your financial plan properly, it will do the same and allow you to create the wealth you and your family deserve.

The hard part about building a house is its design and actual construction. However, once it's built and you move in, you still have to maintain and modify it as time passes. The same is true for your financial plan. That's why it's so important that you have a strong relationship with a financial advisor who can sit down with you on an ongoing basis and help you make any necessary adjustments to your financial plan.

Let's look at the roof on your financial house (your insurance). It's important to have proper protection. You need to have enough property and casualty insurance to protect both your personal and business assets, as well as enough life insurance to cover any liabilities you may have (including future goals, like paying for college). If you don't have the proper protection in place, then you risk losing everything you've worked so hard for. One of the best definitions I've heard is, "Insurance is the transference of risk to an organization that's in the risk-acceptance or risk-management business."

One time, I was talking with a coworker named John and a mentor of ours, and John asked him about getting life insurance. The mentor asked John if he loved his wife. Somewhat surprised, John answered, "Of course I love my wife."

"Then you need to have life insurance."

Fortunately, John listened to our mentor, met with a financial advisor, and got life insurance. A month later, John was killed in a freak accident, and even though his family experienced a great loss, they were financially okay. Had he no life insurance, his wife would've lost their house and taken their children out of their current school district. She would've needed to work, taking time away from the children at a time when they needed her the most.

That was my wake-up call. Even though I didn't have many assets at the time and my wife was already working, I got life insurance. I'm glad that I did, because I was able to lock the insurance in at a lower rate because I was young. As my family grew, I knew I had the proper coverage in case something happened.

When most people begin building their financial foundation, they usually don't have many assets—or a lot of money. If, heaven forbid, something catastrophic happens, they don't have a lot to lose, so they just need the basic necessities. The basic insurance coverage everyone should start out with is

- Auto insurance (if you drive or own a car)
- Homeowner's insurance (if you own a house)
- Renter's insurance (if you are renting)
- Health insurance (at least major medical insurance)

If you're married and are planning on having children in the relatively near future (three to five years), you should also consider getting a small amount of life insurance. You can get more later as you need it. As a business owner, if you don't have health insurance through your job or spouse, there are some high-deductible plans that are relatively inexpensive (note: a deductible is the amount you need to pay out-of-pocket when you file a claim with your insurance company). For example, health insurance for our family of five is $550 a month. There are also ways of purchasing health and even life insurance through your business, and they'll simply become business expenses.

As your financial life becomes more stable, you start to acquire assets, or your family grows, start to increase your insurance coverage to properly protect these new additions. Simultaneously, once your emergency fund is in place, you should create a savings account that will operate as personal insurance for you to use as self-insurance—at least to the level of your deductible. If your deductible is $1,000, for instance, then create a side account where you keep $1,000 (as I discussed with John and Maryann

Smith earlier in the book). It's a good idea to build your insurance account to the point where you can comfortably begin increasing the deductibles on your auto and home/rental policies—and then your health/life insurances themselves.

Most insurance policies have a minimum deductible of $250. From there, they usually move up to a $500 deductible, then $1,000. If there is no way you can come up with $500, then start out with the $250 deductible. I would recommend starting out with a $500 deductible, even if you have to put the deductible on a credit card in emergencies. Unfortunately, if you file an insurance claim, your policy will usually increase by a minimum of 10%. So, if a claim is under $500 (or even $1,000), it would not be worth filing it.

Once you have at least $1,000 saved up in your self-insurance account, increase all of your deductibles to $1,000. You should begin to see a fairly large amount of savings on your insurance policies. As you increase your insurance coverage to protect your multiplying assets—or children—you may want to add these additional coverages:

- **Life Insurance**: Enough to cover your short, mid-, and long-term goals, and (ideally) your family's current standard of living.
- **Disability Insurance**: Enough to cover your monthly living expenses. If your health declines to the point that you can no longer care for yourself and need to enter assisted living, you'll have to pay out-of-pocket until your net worth drops to $2,500 before Medicare kicks in. You could spend your life saving and investing, and without the proper protection in place, you could lose everything. Assisted living can cost your wallet (not your insurance) between $80,000 and $100,000 a year.

When it comes to long-term care, if your net worth is less than $100,000 and you need to spend that down before Medicare kicks in, your estate would take a hit. However, if you're net worth is $450,000, the hit to your estate would be much more significant compared to the cost of insuring long-term care or proper protection. People with a net worth of $500,000 or more are even more vulnerable to having their estates depleted. That said, those most vulnerable have net worths between $100,000 and $500,000.

In the past, long-term care insurance would often cost a lot of money, and if you didn't use it, you would lose it. Nowadays, there are different hybrid long-term care policies. For example, if you pay a set amount down—$100,000—and you need long-term care, the policy will pay out $450,000, allowing you to greatly leverage the $100,000...and if you never need it, you can get the $100,000 back.

As your financial foundation becomes more stable and you are able to implement your larger goals, you can really start enjoying your ideal life style. This is where all your hard work and discipline really start to pay off.

Passive Income

Passive income is money earned from an investment via dividends or interest. Once the passive income from your investments or assets (e.g., income from your business) is at a point where it covers your current or desired lifestyle, you are now financially independent. At this point, you could eliminate disability insurance because you may no longer need it.

Once you're at this point in your plan, re-explore your vision of success. What do you want to accomplish in life? Where do you want to direct your energy? This is probably the most important part of the whole process, as you will keep growing internally while working for and strengthening your financial and business foundation.

Don't move too quickly through this part of the process. If a person saves a lot but ends up getting sick and doesn't have health insurance, he or she could end up spending a good part of their hard-earned money on medical expenses. That person would end up having to start all over again.

No one is immune to unfortunate accidents and mishaps. I knew a man who ran a very successful business, and shortly after he retired, his sixteen-year-old daughter tragically hit and killed a pedestrian. After a lengthy lawsuit, the man lost everything because he didn't have adequate insurance.

Bad things happen to good people, as we all know—and it's very important to have proper coverage for your current situation. I would recommend that, as part of your annual financial review, you always have someone reassess your insurance coverage.

Overall, here are the basic components you should have in place for a rock-solid financial foundation:

- A comprehensive wealth-creation/retirement plan
- Consistently positive net cash flow
- Consistently positive net worth
- A good health insurance policy
- Depending on your age, a long-term care policy
- A life insurance policy large enough to cover your core goals, debt, and ongoing living expenses
- A will or living trust, depending on your situation
- An auto-withdrawal from your general account into your different savings/investment accounts
- A debt-repayment plan (if you have any debt besides your mortgage)
- A succession plan for your business—I will go more into this in the next chapter
- A semiannual assessment of your net worth, preferably with a financial advisor
- A plan for how you will share or give back to others
- An up-to-date estate plan if your net worth, including potential life insurance payouts, are around one million or higher (for estate tax reasons)

In overview, your foundation should be strong enough by this point that you can start truly creating your wealth. Ideally, you have all of your debt paid off (except for maybe your mortgage), which has freed up a lot more disposable income. Hopefully, you also have a good understanding of your goals, dreams, and gifts. New gifting strategies, such as a charitable remainder trust, are also an option at this point. When you are able to incorporate giving into your financial and business plan, things will go even smoother—you can leave a positive mark on humanity and feel a sense of purpose.

With these foundational systems in place, the goal is to keep your investments growing. This will allow you to stay focused on your plan.

Estate Planning

The final step in creating your financial and business plan is to establish an estate or succession plan. It often amazes me how people will work so hard to build a business and accumulate wealth and then lose it through a lack of long-term planning. When creating your estate plan, certain things must be taken into consideration. If you own a business or are self-employed, part of your estate plan should be a succession plan.

A succession plan answers the following questions:

- Who will take over your business if you are unable to work or choose to close the business?
- To whom do you want to leave your estate—meaning, all your assets?
- Do you want your estate broken up and divided among certain people?
- Do you want your business or assets to continue living or performing a job, even after you're no longer here?

Andrew Carnegie (1835 - 1919), who is still considered one of the wealthiest men in the world, set a goal to spend the first half of his life building a fortune and the second half giving it away. He then founded the Carnegie Foundation, which has helped fund libraries, world peace, education, and scientific research. His legacy is Carnegie Hall and contributions of millions of dollars to worthy causes. What will your legacy look like?

"Focus on the journey, not the destination. Joy is found not in finishing an activity, but in doing it."

— *Greg Anderson*

SECTION FOUR

THE JOURNEY HOME

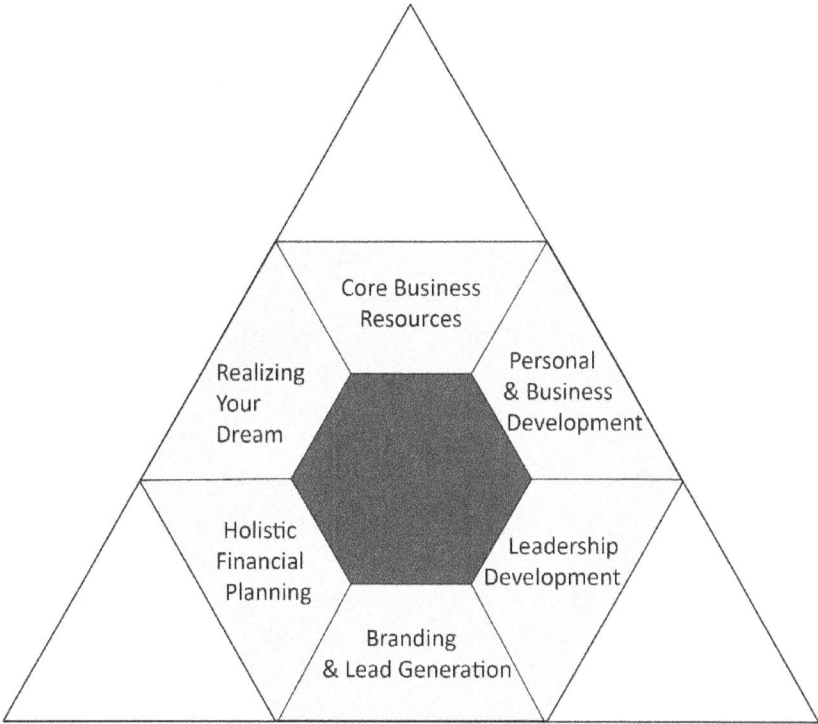

Chapter 19
The Realization of a Dream

Over the years, my family has spoken about how my grandparents were union organizers and how they were always fighting for those around them. They often discussed the weaknesses of capitalism and the evils of big business—and in school, my teachers would talk about the pitfalls of socialism and why it wouldn't ever work.

Growing up, I couldn't help thinking that both had good and bad parts, and if we were able to take the best of both and throw away the rest, we would have an amazing business model. I coined this business model "Social-Capitalism": a business striving to impact and improve the lives of the people it's blessed to work with, and does so without negatively affecting the community around it. It's a business that is designed to support, champion, and empower its members, while continually focusing on streamlining its operations to make a profit.

The day that Sabrina came home from school and said she wanted to design a business that would teach money-management skills to children, I knew that her business would become the seed that my vision would launch from. Over the past eleven years, Sabrina and I have continued to teach children and their parents how to develop a proactive money-management system. Our biggest challenge, however, was that we knew once they mastered the basics, they needed a trusted financial advisor who would help them create a comprehensive financial plan designed around their dreams and goals—and continue to work with them through the process. I had interviewed various people in the financial industry and found that even though there are a lot of great advisors out there, unless a person had a considerable amount of money, it was hard to get the ongoing personal attention that I believed people just starting out needed.

I often thought about getting my financial licenses so that I could better serve our clients and even interviewed with a couple different financial firms. But, at the end of the day, they never seemed like the right fit. I knew that finding the right mix of financial solutions and the business philosophy of creating long-term client-focused relationships was very important, and I knew that until I found the right firm, it would continue to be the missing link in my plan.

Knowing that the right firm would appear when the time was right, I studied as much as I could about business and finances while Sabrina and I kept doing seminars to teach children and their parents the habits and disciplines necessary for developing healthy money-management habits. At night, when the kids were asleep, I worked on the business plan I created when I was twelve, perfecting and expanding the vision.

Over the past thirty-five years, life has moved in many different directions. Often, those who were close to me felt like I was living in my own world—and many times, they were probably right. It was like I had an inner compass leading me from one journey to another. As long as I stayed focused on my dream, one door would shut, closing a chapter, and another one would open. The hard part was that even though I saw those newly opened doors, to those around me, there was nothing there. It was business as usual. So, I would change what I was doing or decide to go somewhere, and it wouldn't make any sense to those around me.

I often looked like I was about to walk off a cliff—figuratively, anyway. I have always been driven by a sense of faith that, in the end, everything will turn out as planned. Even when things hit a roadblock, I knew the answer would show itself. I just needed to remain patient and keep my eyes open for it. It's due to that faith that I have been able to stay on track with my dream over all these years.

With each new change, I attracted the mentors needed at that point in time to move my vision forward. I often felt like I was putting together a large puzzle, and with each passing week, month, and year, the different pieces of the puzzle would be revealed to me. Throughout this book, I have shared stories of how, every now and then, something would happen that would change my course of direction, yet the dream always stayed out in front.

As a teenager, I was able to lay the seeds for my dream or business plan. Over the five years I was in Taiwan (where I met my wife), I was able to meet and learn from many different mentors. I would often journal about the trip and my business plan, and I created my very first Dream Board there. After returning to the states, Jennifer and I stopped in Seattle (intending to stay only two weeks), and we ended up remaining there for sixteen years.

I knew shortly after landing in Seattle that there were things I needed to learn there before I would be ready to return home. It also seemed like a great place for Jennifer to begin her journey in America. I just didn't know how long it would take. And my limousine company became a great classroom for learning how to build a business—plus I could talk to and learn from many of my clients over the years.

The vision I had when I was a child became clearer and clearer, yet it still had missing components. I knew that it would grow into a large organization and would serve as an incubator for small to midsized businesses, giving them the tools needed to get to the next level—an environment to support them so they could focus on their core plans. I also knew that in order for the vision to be a success, it needed to be made up of different divisions, and that would take the help of many different people. The greatest challenge over time has been recognizing when I reached the end of one road and when it was time to go in a different direction. I believe that there are things or events in our lives that serve as markers, showing us that we are on the right path, or that it's time to change directions.

At times, an experience will create an anchor to draw us back to that point or place at a later time. The problem is that they will often go unnoticed unless we are paying attention to them.

I will share one such example—an anchor that has become very important, because without it, things would be radically different now. I was fifteen and living with my dad in Waukesha, Wisconsin, on Grandville Drive. My last night there ended in a huge argument with my dad. He told me he didn't want me there anymore and that I needed to move back to Milwaukee with my mom.

When leaving his front yard and getting into my mom's car, I told myself that someday I would return and make things right. The anchor was laid. My dad and I didn't talk for a year or two after that. Later that fall, he sold his house and moved to Indiana. For years, I never thought about Grandville Drive, but the anchor was still there in the background, waiting to resurface.

Thirty years later, and after a couple of really hard months of soul-searching, I dropped to my knees in frustration and called out in prayer, "Please, God, if I'm on the wrong path, tell me what to do and I'll do it. But, if I am supposed to continue working on my vision, and if that vision is to help children, parents, and small-business owners develop a solid financial and business foundation...then please, please open a door for that to happen."

The next morning I was to give a speech for Toastmasters on goal-setting, but at the last minute, I had a strong feeling that I needed to talk about becoming financially independent instead. I changed my speech at the last minute. Having only five minutes to redo it, I put my speech on goal-setting down, got up, and spoke from the heart. After Toastmasters was over, one of the members of the club came up to me and said, "I was really impressed by your passion for helping people get their finances in order." He then asked, "Are you in the financial business?"

I said, "No, but I often think about it."

He then told me, "I was really busy at work and wasn't going to come to Toastmasters this morning, but I had a strong feeling at the last minute that I needed to be here. So I jumped in the car and came."

After hearing my speech, he realized why he needed to be there. He then said, "We're having an open house at my office and I would like to invite you." I went to his office, and for the first time in many years, I had the overwhelming feeling that I was home.

I didn't understand why, but everything felt so comfortable—as if I had been there before. A week later, after joining the firm, I was leaving an appointment I had about a mile from the office. I made a left turn and started up a hill to the road that went back to the office. I pulled over in amazement. There it was, right in front of me: my dad's old house. Tears started to stream down my face. Memory after memory surfaced as if they were on fast forward.

Wiping the tears from my face, I reached down picked up my phone and dialed my dad's number.

"Hello?" my dad answered.

"Hi, Dad. It's me. I'm sitting in front of the Grandville house, and I just wanted to say how sorry I am for being such a punk back then."

"Hey, kiddo, don't worry about it. You were just being a normal fifteen-year-old kid, stuck in a situation you didn't want or ask to be in. I'm sorry, too, for not being there when you needed me."

We talked for a while, and after we hung up, I felt this incredible sense of peace come over me. I started to laugh as I realized that my new office was on Grandville drive, one mile from my dad's old house. And I even developed a friendship with a guy in the firm who lived around the corner from where my dad lived. Is it just a small world? Or something more?

I'm not sure how, but the anchor from the night of our fight created a void that was filled when I went to the open house at my friend's office. It made joining his firm a very natural move. The reason for our move back to Milwaukee was there in front of me. I was now in the financial business, and I was on my way to completing the final stage of the dream I'd had all those years.

My friend from Toastmasters and two of the leaders in the office had become mentors to me. The people in the office clearly cared about their clients and were passionate about helping other people move toward creating financial independence. Every Tuesday, we would have training from 6:30 to 8:30. People would talk about how they were impacting their clients and trying to always put the client first. I loved being there. Yet, for some reason, things still didn't feel quite right.

I was very confused and found myself regularly praying for guidance. I believed that, above all else, they were the mentors I needed to complete my dream, yet the energy somehow still didn't feel right. I knew that even though my and Sabrina's Children and Beyond program was about teaching kids money-management skills and helping their parents become financially independent, the firm could not yet deliver the foundation my vision needed.

I hoped that if I continued to grow myself and build a strong business, everything would fall into place at the right time. I knew that together we could accomplish amazing things, but some aspects would have to change first. I did not know that they were also on the same quest.

At a point when I once again started to question my path, they shared with us their own challenges, and that they had also been looking for a better way. It became even clearer why I met them and that they held the key to the final stage in implementing my dream—which was, in fact, a mutual dream.

That day, Dean and Dina at the firm announced that they were going to pursue their dream of creating a financial firm that was completely independent from outside influences, so it could always put the clients' needs first. It would be a firm designed to make a radical difference in the way financial planning was done. Over the next year, everything started to fall into place, and Global View Capital Advisors was born.

I will be forever grateful for all that Dean and Dina Fliss have taught me. The new firm indeed became the final piece of my vision's puzzle.

I have shared through this book what my dream is. I shared what an influence that Brian Buffini and Buffini & Company has been in my life. Without their help, I probably wouldn't be writing this now. I am also eternally grateful for what Dean and Dina Fliss have taught me, all they do for us within the Global View Capital family, and those we are blessed to be able to serve.

The creation of this dream has been a journey and has required the help of many people along the way. There have been many challenges as well as many great days, and I look forward to what the future will bring.

As I bring this story to an end, I would like to thank everyone who has helped me, and I am honored to call you my mentors and friends. I invite you to join me on this journey. The dream and the future have become today. Together, let's change the world into the place it was designed to be!

About the Author

Mike Raber is a business/financial consultant, Father, speaker and author. Over the last 35 years, he has started and built various businesses, giving him a great understanding of the different stages a business will go through, and the importance of building a strong foundation equipped to handle the many challenges a business will go through.

Mike has trained many entrepreneurs how to grow their businesses, and alongside his children, had shared many financial management and goal setting skills to hundreds of children and their parents. From these different ventures he has continued to gain experience in the business and financial world allowing him to help other entrepreneurs bring their passions or ideas to life. Empowering them to start and grow their businesses.

Mike currently lives in Wisconsin with his wife and three children. As his children have grown over the years, Mike has brought many of the stories and lesson learned about business and finances home and shared them with his children. His daughter Sabrina started her own company at the age of nine teaching kids core money management skills and, at the age of 18, she co-authored a book with Mike named "Parenting That Makes Cents: The Secret to Raising Financially Savvy Kids." This became the launching pad for their book and speaking series "Centsible Solutions."

If you would like to learn more about this book serious, or if you would like to have Mike speak at one of your events, Go to www.entrepreneurshipthatmakescents.com for more information.